Strategies proven to work.

Content instruction created just for the Upper Level SSAT. Practice to reinforce learning.

✓ Strategies to use for each section of the Upper Level SSAT

✓ Content instruction specific to the test and age-appropriate

✓ Drills and practice sets to build skills and confidence

✓ Full-length practice tests to show students what to expect and avoid surprises on test day (*Success on the Upper Level SSAT* and *The Best Unofficial Practice Tests* only)

Complete selection of Upper Level SSAT titles now available from Test Prep Works LLC:

Success on the Upper Level SSAT: A Complete Course
- Strategies for each section of the test
- Reading and vocabulary drills
- In-depth math content instruction with practice sets
- 1 full-length practice test

30 Days to Acing the Upper Level SSAT
- Strategies for each section of the test
- Fifteen "workouts", each providing practice problems and detailed explanations for every section of the test
- Perfect for additional practice or homework

The Best Unofficial Practice Tests for the Upper Level SSAT
- 2 additional full-length practice tests

30 DAYS
TO *Acing* THE
Upper Level SSAT

Strategies and Practice for Maximizing Your Upper Level SSAT Score

Christa Abbott, M.Ed.

Published by:
Test Prep Works, LLC
PO Box 100572
Arlington, VA 22210
www.TestPrepWorks.com

For information about buying this title in bulk, or for editions with customized covers or content, please contact us at sales@testprepworks.com or (703) 944-6727.

SSAT is a registered trademark of the Secondary School Admission Test Board. They have not endorsed nor are they associated with this book.

Neither the author nor the publisher of this book claims responsibility for the accuracy of this book or the outcome of students who use these materials.

ISBN 978-1-939090-20-1

Contents

About the Author

Christa Abbott has been a private test prep tutor for over a decade. She has worked with students who have been admitted to and attended some of the top independent schools in the country. Over the years, she has developed materials for each test that truly make the difference.

Christa is a graduate of Middlebury College and received her Masters in Education from the University of Virginia, a program nationally known for its excellence. Her background in education allows her to develop materials based on the latest research about how we learn so that preparation can be an effective and efficient use of time. Her materials are also designed to be developmentally appropriate for the ages of the students taking the tests. In her free time, she enjoys hiking, tennis, Scrabble, and reading. Her greatest joy is spending time with her husband and three children.

Christa continues to work with students one-on-one in the Washington, D.C., area. She also works with students internationally via Skype. If you are interested in these services, please visit www.ChristaAbbott.com.

About Test Prep Works, LLC

Test Prep Works, LLC, was founded to provide effective materials for test preparation. Its founder, Christa Abbott, spent years looking for effective materials for the private school entrance exams but came up empty-handed. The books available combined several different tests and while there are overlaps, they are not the same test. Christa found this to be very overwhelming for students who were in elementary and middle school and that just didn't seem necessary. Christa developed her own materials to use with students that are specific for each level of the test and are not just adapted from other books. For the first time, these materials are available to the general public as well as other tutors. Our titles include the *Success* series of complete coursebooks, the *30 Days* series of practice books, and the *Best Unofficial Practice Tests* series with additional full-length practice tests. Please visit *www.testprepworks.com* to view all of our offerings and to sign up for our newsletter with recent news and developments in the world of admissions and test preparation.

How to Use This Book

This book is designed to teach you what you need to know in order to maximize your Upper Level SSAT performance. The book starts with a brief introduction to strategies for each section. After that, there is a series of "workouts". Each of these workouts should take about 30 minutes.

Within each workout, I have included strategy and practice for each section so that you get a "balanced diet" leading up to test day. You will notice some repetition – this is by design! In particular, you may see vocabulary words or words with the same roots repeated. This is to ensure that you don't forget the vocabulary that you have already studied. After you complete each workout, be sure to check your answers and figure out WHY you missed the questions that you did. The analysis is as important as the answers themselves.

I have spent years studying the test and analyzing the different question types, content, and the types of answers that test writers prefer. Now you can benefit from my hard work! First, work through the strategy sections at the beginning of the book. The workouts will then reinforce these strategies as well as expose you to new vocabulary and content.

Let's get started!

P.S. I chose not to go into the nitty-gritty details in this book about how to register, what to bring on test day, etc., because I want you to focus on strategies and practice for now. Make sure to visit *www.ssat.org* to get all of the current details on registration and other procedures. I also highly recommend ordering their practice book, *The Official Guide to the Upper Level SSAT*. It has two practice tests in it that you can complete after you finish all of the workouts.

P.P.S. If you are looking for additional Upper Level SSAT resources such as practice tests or content instruction, please visit *www.testprepworks.com* for more information on our other materials, including *Success on the Upper Level SSAT: A Complete Course* and *The Best Unofficial Practice Tests for the Upper Level SSAT*.

The 30 Days to SSAT Success Game Plan

Step 1: Read through the strategies section of this book.

Take the time to really understand each strategy, and know that what you have learned will be reinforced in the workouts.

Step 2: Complete the workouts.

When you miss a question, take the time to understand WHY you missed it before you move on to the next workout. Make flashcards for words or roots that you don't know and study them as you go.

Step 3: Read the appendix.

It gives advice on how to tackle the writing sample.

Step 4: Take the practice tests.

Order the book *The Official Guide to the Upper Level SSAT*. (Please note that the ONLY place you can get this book is from *www.ssat.org*). Take the Upper Level practice tests using the strategies that you have learned. Understand why you missed the questions that you did.

Other practice tests are available in addition to the ones in the official guide, including three that Test Prep Works has developed. Two are found in *The Best Unofficial Practice Tests for the Upper Level SSAT*, and a third is included at the back of *Success on the Upper Level SSAT: A Complete Course*.

Step 5: Rock the SSAT!

What You Need to Know for the SSAT — Just the Basics

How the scoring works

On the Upper Level SSAT, if you answer a question correctly, then you are given one point. If you answer a question incorrectly, then a quarter point is deducted. If you don't answer at all, then you don't get a point added to your raw score, but nothing is deducted either.

You might be asking why they use this crazy system. The thinking behind it is that on a regular test, you would get ahead by guessing. You would answer some of the questions that you guessed on correctly and therefore your score would be higher for blindly guessing. Chances are that you would answer one-fifth of the questions correctly if you blindly guessed, because there are five answer choices for each question. By taking off a quarter point for the four-fifths of the questions that you miss, the test writers are making sure that you don't get ahead for blindly guessing.

When to guess

You should only guess if you can rule out at least one answer choice.

The percentile score

You will get a raw score for the SSAT based upon how many questions you answered correctly or incorrectly. This raw score will then be converted into a scaled score. Neither of these scores is what schools are really looking at. They are looking for your percentile scores, and in particular the percentile scores that compare you to other students applying to independent school.

- Percentile score is what schools are really looking at

The percentile score compares you to other students of the same gender who are in your grade. For example, let's say that you are an eighth grade boy and scored in the 70th percentile. What this means is that out of 100 boys in your grade, you did better than 70 of them.

- Your percentile score compares you only to other students in your grade

Keep in mind that the Upper Level SSAT is given to students up through 11th grade. That means that if you are taking the test in 8th grade, there could very well be some material on the test that you simply have not yet covered. You may miss some of these questions, but as long as the other students your age also miss them, then it won't affect your percentile score.

- You may miss more questions than you are used to, but that is OK as long as other students your age also miss those questions

Many students applying to independent schools are used to answering almost all of the questions on a test correctly. You will probably miss more questions on this test than you are used to missing, but don't let it get to you because the percentile score is what schools are looking at.

The Format of the Upper Level SSAT

You can expect to see four scored sections *plus* a writing sample *plus* an experimental section on the Upper Level SSAT.

The four scored sections

- Quantitative (two of these sections will be on your test)
    - ✓ A variety of math problems
    - ✓ Each section has 25 problems, for a total of 50 math problems
    - ✓ 30 minutes to complete each section, or a little more than a minute per problem

- Verbal
    - ✓ 30 synonym questions and 30 analogy questions
    - ✓ 30 minutes to complete the section, or about 30 seconds per question

- Reading Comprehension
    - ✓ Passages and questions
    - ✓ Passages can be fiction, non-fiction, and poetry
    - ✓ A total of 40 questions
    - ✓ Generally 6-8 passages, each passage having 4-8 questions, but this is not carved in stone so you may see some variation
    - ✓ 40 minutes to complete section

The four sections above are multiple-choice. Each question has five answer choices.

The experimental section

- 16 questions with 15 minutes to complete
- Will NOT contribute to your score
- SSATB is just trying out new problems for future tests, not to worry

The writing sample

- Will NOT be scored, but a copy will be sent to all of the schools that you apply to
- You will be able to choose one of two writing prompts – one will be fiction and one will be an essay
- 25 minutes to write and you will be given two pages to write on

Now, on to the strategies! The strategies covered in this book will focus on the multiple-choice sections since those are what is used to determine your percentile. Please see the appendix for tips on the essay before test day.

The Mother of All Strategies

Use the process of elimination, or "ruling out"

If you remember nothing else on test day, remember to use the process of elimination. This is a multiple-choice test, and there are often answers that don't even make sense.

When you read a question, you should read all of the answer choices before selecting one. You need to keep in mind that the test will ask you to choose the answer choice that "best" answers the question. Best is a relative word, so how can you know which answer choice best answers the question if you don't read them all?

- After you read the question, read ALL of the answer choices
- Look for the "best" answer, which may be the least wrong answer choice

After you have read all of the answer choices, rule them out in order from most wrong to least wrong. Sometimes the "best" answer choice is not a great fit, but it is better than the others. This process will also clarify your thinking so that by the time you get down to only two answer choices, you have a better idea of what makes choices right or wrong.

- Rule out in order from most wrong to least wrong

Above all else, remember that you are playing the odds on this test. To increase your score, you need to answer questions even when you are not positive of the answer.

Verbal Section – Basic Strategies

In the verbal section you will see two question types:

- Synonyms
- Analogies

On the synonyms questions, you will be given one question word and then you have to choose the answer choice that has the word that comes closest in meaning to the question word.

Synonyms questions look something like this:

1. JOYOUS:
   - (A) loud
   - (B) crying
   - (C) happy
   - (D) shy
   - (E) lame

   Out of all the answer choice words, happy comes closest in meaning to joyous. Choice C is correct.

The synonyms questions probably won't be quite this easy, but you get the idea.

The analogies questions generally give you two words and you have to figure out the relationship between them and then choose the answer choice that has the same relationship.

The analogies questions usually look something like this:

1. Panther is to cat as

    (A) lion is to jungle
    (B) wolf is to dog
    (C) chick is to blue jay
    (D) mouse is to guinea pig
    (E) horse is to cow

In this case, a panther is a wild cat. A wolf is a wild dog, so choice B is correct.

Sometimes, you will be given the first word in the answer relationship and then you have to choose the second word.

These questions look like this:

2. Tall is to short as narrow is to

    (A) long
    (B) square
    (C) wide
    (D) measured
    (E) lax

Tall and short are opposites, so we are looking for the answer choice that is the opposite of narrow. Wide is the opposite of narrow, so choice C is correct.

Since synonyms and analogies questions are very different, we use different strategies for them.

Synonyms strategies

The synonyms strategies are:

- Come up with your own word
- Think of a sentence or phrase in which you have heard the word
- Use positive or negative
- Look for any roots or word parts that you recognize
- If you have to guess, see if there is an answer choice that has the same prefix, suffix, or root as the question word

Strategy #1: Come up with your own word

Use this strategy when you read through a sentence and a word just pops into your head. Don't force yourself to come up with your own definition when you aren't sure what the word means.

If you read a question word and a synonym pops into your head, go ahead and jot it down. It is important that you write down the word because otherwise you may try to talk yourself into an answer choice that "seems to come close". One of the biggest enemies on any standardized test is doubt. Doubt leads to talking yourself into the wrong answer, and physically writing down the word gives you the confidence you need when you go through the answer choices.

After you write down the word, start by crossing out answer choices that are not synonyms for your word. By the time you get down to two choices, you will have a much better idea of what you are looking for.

Strategy #2: Use context – Think of where you have heard the word before

Use this strategy when you can't define a word, but you can think of a sentence or phrase in which you have heard the word before.

Here is how it works: Think of a sentence or phrase in which you have heard the question word before. Then try plugging the answer choices into your phrase to see which one has the same meaning within that sentence or phrase.

Here is an example:

1. SHIRK:

    (A) rush
    (B) send
    (C) learn
    (D) avoid
    (E) clutter

Now let's say you have heard the word "shirk" but can't define it. You remember your mom telling you "don't shirk your responsibilities" when you tried to watch TV before your chores were done. So we plug in the answer choices for the word "shirk" in your sentence. Does it make sense to say "don't rush your responsibilities"? It might make sense, but it wouldn't have the same meaning as your context. You weren't in trouble for rushing your chores, you were in trouble for not doing them at all so we can rule out choice A. Does it make sense to say "don't send your responsibilities"? Not at all. Choice B is out. Does "don't learn your responsibilities" work? Nope, choice C is out. Would your mom say "don't avoid your responsibilities"? You bet. Choice D is correct.

Sometimes the only word or phrase that you can think of uses a different form of the word. That is OK as long as you change the answer choices when you plug in.

Here is an example:

2. CHERISH:

    (A) treasure
    (B) enforce
    (C) utter
    (D) concern
    (E) calm

Maybe you have heard your English teacher talk about Little Women as "one of my most cherished books." We can use that context, we just have to add the "-ed" to the answer choices when we plug them in. Does it make sense to say "one of my most treasured books"? Yes it does, so we will keep choice A. Would "one of my most enforced books" work? No, so we can rule out choice B. What about "one of my most uttered books" or "one of my most concerned books" or "one of my most calmed books"? No, no, and no, so we rule out choices C, D, and E. Choice A is correct.

Strategy #3: Use positive or negative

Sometimes you see a word, and you can't define that word, but you have a "gut feeling" that it is either something good or something bad. Maybe you don't know what that word means, but you know you would be mad if someone called you that!

To use this strategy, when you get that feeling that a word is either positive or negative, then write in a "+" or a "–" sign next to the word. Then go to your answer choices and rule out anything that is opposite, i.e., positive when your question word is negative or negative when your question word is positive.

To really make this strategy work for you, you also need to rule out any words that are neutral, or neither positive nor negative. For example, let's say the question word is DISTRESS. Distress is clearly a negative word. So we can rule out a positive answer choice, such as friendly, but we can also rule out a neutral word, such as sleepy. At night, it is good to be sleepy, during the day it is not. Sleepy is not clearly a negative word, so it goes.

Here is an example:

1. CONDEMN:
   (A) arrive
   (B) blame
   (C) tint
   (D) favor
   (E) laugh

Let's say that you know that condemn is bad, but you can't think of a definition. We write a "–" sign next to it and then rule out anything that is positive. That means that choices D and E can go because they are both positive. Now we can also rule out neutral words because we know that condemn is negative. Arrive and tint are neither positive nor negative, so choices A and C are out. We are left with choice B, which is correct.

Strategy #4: Look for roots or word parts that you know

This strategy works when you recognize that a word looks like another word you know or when you recognize one of the roots that you have studied in school or in the workouts in this book.

If you see something familiar in the question word, underline the roots or word parts that you recognize. If you can think of the meaning of the root, then look for answer choices that go with that meaning. If you can't think of a specific meaning, think of other words that have that root and look for answer choices that are similar in meaning to those other words.

1. EXCLUDE:
    (A) prohibit
    (B) feel
    (C) rest
    (D) drift
    (E) rejoice

There are two word parts in the word "exclude" that can help us out. First, we have the prefix "ex-", which means out (think of the word "exit"). Secondly, "clu" is a word root that means to shut (think of the word "include"). Using these word parts, we can see that exclude has something to do with shutting out. Choice A comes closest to this meaning, so it is correct.

Strategy #5: Guess an answer choice with the same prefix, suffix, or word root as the question word

If nothing else, see if any of the answer choices have the same root, prefix, or suffix (a suffix is an ending on a word). You would be amazed how many of the correct answers have the same root as the question word.

Let's look at the following example:

1. PERMISSIBLE:
    (A) edible
    (B) crazy
    (C) strong
    (D) allowable
    (E) gentle

Even if you don't know what permissible means, the "-ible" ending tells us that it must mean able to do something. The "-ible" and "-able" suffixes have the same meaning, so we could guess between choices A and D. Edible means able to be eaten, but allowable is a synonym for permissible, so choice D is correct.

Analogies strategies

The strategies for analogies are:

- If you know the question words, make a sentence
- If you don't know one of the question words, head to the answer choices
- If you get stuck on the last ten analogies, guess the weirdest answer choices

Strategy #1: Make a sentence from the question words

To use this strategy, you have to at least have a vague sense of what both question words mean. Basically, you make a sentence from the question words and then plug answer choices into that sentence to see which answer choice has the same relationship.

Here is an example:

1. Water is to ocean as

    (A) cloud is to sky
    (B) mountain is to hill
    (C) paint is to watercolor
    (D) ice is to glaciers
    (E) sneaker is to marathon

If we make a sentence from the question words, we might say "water makes up the ocean". Now we plug in our answer choices, subbing in the answer words for the question words. Does it make sense to say "cloud makes up the sky"? Sometimes that is true, but if we have to use the word "sometimes", then it is not a strong relationship so we can rule out choice A. Does a "mountain make up a hill"? No, so choice B is gone. Does "paint make up a watercolor"? That doesn't make sense, so we can rule out choice C. Does "ice make up glaciers"? Yes. Choice D is correct. We would keep going and plug in choice E just to make sure that it wasn't a better fit, but choice D is correct.

There are several relationships that show up frequently on the SSAT. If you become familiar with them, it makes it much easier to make up your own sentences quickly.

They are:

1. Occupation – one word is the job of the other word
    Example: Architect is to building

2. Part of – one word is a part of the other word
    Example: Kitchen is to house

3. Type of – one word is a type of the other word, which is a broader category
    Example: Whale is to mammal

4. Used for – one word is used to do the other word
    Example: Shovel is to dig

5. Degree – the words have roughly the same meaning, only one is more extreme
    Example: Hungry is to starving

6. Characteristic of – one word is a characteristic of the other
    Example: Massive is to elephant

7. Synonyms – the words are synonyms
    Example: Deceitful is to dishonest

8. Antonyms – the words are opposite in meaning
    Example: Friendly is to rude

9. Found in – one word is found in the other
    Example: Shark is to ocean

10. Grammatical – one word has a grammatical relationship to the other
    Example: Meet is to met

Strategy #2: If you don't know one of the question words, head to the answer choices

If you read through the question words and don't know what one (or more!) of the question words means, all is not lost. Try to make sentences with the answer choices. Sometimes there are answer choices with words that are not even related. Rule these out. Then plug the question words into the sentences you made from the remaining answer choices and see if they could work. Rule out any that don't. Guess from what you have left.

Keep in mind that if you find yourself using words like "could", "maybe", "can", or "sometimes", it is not a strong relationship so you should rule it out.

Here is an example:

1. (Weird word) is to ship as

    (A) luck is to delay
    (B) fun is to laughter
    (C) helmet is to football
    (D) mansion is to house
    (E) first is to last

Since we don't know one of the question words, we go to the answers. If we try to make a sentence from choice A, we can see that luck and delay don't have a strong relationship. You could say that if you are lucky, you might not have a delay. However, that would be talking yourself into a relationship isn't strong at all (if you have to use words like "sometimes", "might", "may", or "could", it is not a good relationship). Choice A is out. For choice B, you could say that laughter is the result of fun. However, if we plug the question words back into that sentence, is there anything that ship is a result of? Not really, so we can rule out choice B. If we look at choice C, you could say that that a helmet is worn to play football. But if we plug our question words into that sentence, is there anything that is worn to play ship? No. Choice C is out. On to choice D. A mansion is a type of house. Could something be a type of ship? Absolutely, so we keep choice D. Finally, choice E. First and last are opposites. But is there a word that means the opposite of ship? No, so choice E is out. We were able to narrow it down to one choice (choice D) without even knowing one of the question words.

Strategy #3: If you get stuck on any of the last ten analogies, guess the weirdest answer choices

The questions on this test go from easy to most difficult. Most students miss the last questions. However, most students REFUSE to guess words that they don't know. You know what this means, right? It means that if you want to raise your percentile score, you have to guess the answer choice that most students aren't going to guess.

Try to read through the answer choices in your head. The more difficulty you have pronouncing the words, the more likely it is to be the right answer choice on the last part of the analogies section. This isn't an exact science, but it works often enough that you will come out ahead.

For example, let's say you guess the weirdest words on the last ten analogies and only get half of them correct. You get 5 points for the five that you answered correctly, and you only lose 1.25 points for the five that you missed. You come out ahead.

Those are the basic strategies for the synonyms and analogies. The other important piece of improving your verbal score is studying vocabulary. The workouts will help you with that, but you should also make flashcards for words that you run across that you do not know.

Reading Comprehension Section – Basic Strategies

The reading section consists of passages and questions. You can expect to see fiction, non-fiction, and poetry. The number of passages per test varies, but there tends to be 6-8 passages with 4-8 questions each. There will always be a total of 40 questions in the section, however.

The basic strategies for the reading comprehension section are:

- Before you read, go to the questions. If it is a general question (about the whole passage), mark it with a "G". If it is a specific question, mark it with an "S" and then underline either the line reference or the key word of what it is asking about.
- After you mark the questions, go ahead and read.
- Answer specific questions first. If you can't underline the correct answer in the passage (reworded), then you haven't found it yet – keep looking!
- To answer general questions, reread the last sentence.

Strategy #1: Before you read, mark the questions with "S" or "G"

It is important that you identify specific (S) and general (G) questions before you begin to read. You may come across the answer to a specific question as you read, so you also want to underline what the question is asking about for specific questions.

So how do you know if it is specific or general?

Here are some examples of the forms that specific questions often take:

- In the first paragraph, the word _____ means
- In line 5, _____ means
- In line 7, _____ most likely refers to
- All of the following are mentioned EXCEPT
- All of the following questions are answered EXCEPT

If there is a line reference or the question has a lot of details, then it is probably a specific question.

If there is a line reference, go ahead and put a mark next to that line in the passage. That way you will know to go answer that question when you are reading. If the question asks about a specific detail, underline what it asks about so that you know what to look for when you read.

For example, let's say our question was:

1. How many years did it take Johnny Appleseed to plant his trees?

We would underline the word "years" since that is the detail we are looking for. Presumably, the whole passage would be about him planting trees, so that would not be a helpful detail to look for.

Some questions may look general, but on the SSAT they are looking for a specific example.

Here is how these questions may look:

- The author would most likely agree
- Which of the following questions is answered by the passage?
- According to the passage/author
- It can be inferred from the passage
- This passage infers/implies which of the following

The reason that these questions are specific is that on the SSAT the answers to these questions will be found in a single sentence or two. In real life that may not be true, but on this test it is. We can't underline anything for these questions, however, since the details we are looking for are in the answer choices.

General questions ask about the passage as a whole. They might look like:

- This passage primarily deals with
- This passage is mainly about
- The main purpose of this passage is to
- Which of the following best expresses the author's main point?
- What is the best title of this passage?
- The author's tone is
- The author's attitude is

If you see words like "mainly" or "primarily" you have a general question on your hands and should mark it with a "G".

Please keep in mind that you do not have to be correct every time when you mark "S" or "G". Do not obsess over whether a question is specific or general. The point of this strategy is to save you time and it isn't that big of a deal if you mark one question incorrectly.

Strategy #2: After you mark the questions, go ahead and read

As you read, keep an eye out for answers to specific questions. Don't read too slowly or feel like you need to memorize every sentence. If you come across a section that answers a question, then you slow down and read very, very carefully. There is no point in obsessing over material that there are no questions about, however.

Strategy #3: Answer specific questions first

The deal with specific questions is that you can find the answer restated in the passage. Always. If you haven't found it, then you need to keep looking.

There are a few secrets to dealing with the specific reading questions. They are:

Secret #1: Answers to specific questions are very detail-oriented

Often the answers to questions can be found in just a word or two out of the whole passage. Also, the questions are not necessarily in the order of the passage. The way to overcome this problem is to read the questions before reading the passage. That way, you know what you are looking for.

Secret #2: The test writers twist words from the passage around so that answer choices have the same words but different meanings

For example, the passage may say that "John was upset when Sam got into the car with Trish."

The question may look something like:

1. Which of the following is implied by the author?
   - (A) John was upset with Trish when Sam drove the car.
   - (B) John was upset with Trish when he got into the car.
   - (C) Sam and Trish were upset when John got into the car.
   - (D) John and Sam are cousins.
   - (E) John was not happy because Sam rode with Trish.

   Choices A, B, and C use words from the passage, but the order is switched around so that the meanings are different. Choice E restates what the passage says using different words that have the same meaning. That is what we are looking for.

To avoid making a mistake, watch out for answers that repeat exact words from the passage. Answers that repeat words aren't always wrong, but should be carefully analyzed to make sure that the meaning isn't twisted.

Secret #3: Our brain fills in words that simply are not there

As we read, we automatically fill in details. For example, let's say that the passage says:

"Samuel came from a family of enormous height – it was said that even his mother was six feet four inches tall."

The question might then look like:

1. Which of the following about Samuel can be inferred from the passage?
   - (A) He is well educated.
   - (B) He is very tall.
   - (C) His favorite pastime is basketball.
   - (D) He left school at an early age.
   - (E) He was the first astronaut to be a pet owner.

As we read, our mind probably filled in that Samuel is tall since the passage says that his family was tall. However, the passage does NOT say that Samuel is tall. Odds are good that we won't remember this, however, since our mind has already filled in the blank. We would choose choice B, even though it is incorrect.

The way that we overcome this is by underlining the evidence in the passage for the correct answer choice for specific questions. Every. Single. Time. If you can't underline the answer, you haven't found it yet.

If you remember to apply these secrets, you should ace the specific questions.

Strategy #4: Before answering general questions, reread the last sentence of the entire passage

On the SSAT, you want to answer general questions last. The reason we do this is that by the time that you have answered all of the specific questions, you generally have read the passage several times.

One hazard of having looked at all the details of a passage closely is that we sometimes lose sight of the main idea. If we reread the last sentence before answering general questions, it will keep us focused on the main idea.

Often, several of the answer choices for general questions will be details from the passage. You might be able to find evidence for that answer in the passage, but it will be wrong because this is a general question and NOT a specific one! Look for the answer choice that comes closest in meaning to the very last sentence of the entire passage.

Quantitative Sections – Basic Strategies

On the quantitative sections, there are problems from arithmetic, algebra, and geometry. The math is really not that hard. The SSAT is more about figuring out what concepts they are testing than remembering complicated equations.

You will NOT be allowed to use a calculator on the SSAT. By using strategies, however, we often can get to the right answers without using complicated calculations.

The goal of this section is to give you a general understanding of the key strategies for the math section. You will practice these strategies and work on content in the workouts.

Drumroll, please! The strategies are:

- Estimate – this is a multiple-choice test!
- If there are variables in the answer choices, try plugging in your own numbers
- If a question asks for the value of a variable, plug in answer choices
- If you can, find a range that the answer should fall within

Strategy #1: Estimate

You can spend a lot of time finding the exact right answer on this test, or you can spend time figuring out which answers couldn't possibly work and then choosing from what is left.

For example, let's say the question is:

1. $72,341 \div 2,281 =$

    The answer to above equation is closest to which of the following?

    (A) 72,000
    (B) 70,000
    (C) 36,000
    (D) 360
    (E) 36

If you were to do out the whole problem, that would take a long time without a calculator. However, if we look at our answer choices, we can see that most of them are pretty spread out. We just need to know roughly what the answer is, so we can do 72,000 ÷ 2,000, which gives us 36, or answer choice E.

You can estimate on many of the problems, but be sure to do so when the question uses the words "closest to" or "approximately".

Strategy #2: Plug in your own numbers if there are variables in the answer choices

What do I mean by variables in the answer choices? If you look at the answer choices and some or all of them have letters in addition to numbers, then you have variables in your answer choices.

Here is how this strategy works:

Step 1: Plug in your own numbers.

Make up your own numbers for the variables. Just make sure they work within the problem. If they say that x is less than 1, do not make x equal to 2! If they say $x + y = 1$, then for heaven's sake, don't make x equal to 2 and y equal to 3. Also, make sure that you write down what you are plugging in for your variables. EVERY TIME. You think you will remember that x was 4, but then you go to try out answer choices and it gets all confused. Just write it down the first time. Also, try to avoid using -1, 1, and 0 because they have funky properties and you might get more than one answer that works. The exception to this rule is when the question asks you what *must* be true. In that case, you want to use the funky numbers to try to rule out answer choices.

Step 2: Solve using your own numbers.

Write down the number that you get and circle it. This is the number you are trying to get with your answer choices when you plug in your value for the variable.

Step 3: Plug into answer choices.

Plug the numbers that you assigned to the variables in step 1 into the answer choices and see which answer choice matches the number that you circled.

Here is an example:

1. Each mama mouse can have up to 9 baby mice in a litter. What is the maximum total number of mice that could wind up in a cage if there are x mama mice in the cage?

   (A) $x + 9$
   (B) $9x$
   (C) $9x + 9$
   (D) $10x$
   (E) $10x + 10$

Step 1: Plug in your own number.

Let's make x equal to 3. We now have 3 mama mice.

Step 2: Solve using your own numbers.

If we have 3 mama mice, and they could each have 9 babies, then the total number of mice we could wind up with in our cage is 30. We write down this number and circle it.

Step 3: Plug into answer choices.

We are looking for the answer choice that is equal to 30.

   (A) $3 + 9 = 12$
   (B) $9(3) = 27$
   (C) $9(3) + 9 = 36$
   (D) $10(3) = 30$
   (E) $10(3) + 10 = 40$

Choice D gives us 30, which is what we were looking for, so we choose D and answer the question correctly.

If the question asks you which answer choice is greatest or least, then you won't come up with a target number to circle. Rather, you will plug your values into the answer choices and see which one is greatest or least, depending on what the question asked for.

Here is an example:

2. If x is less than 0, and y is greater than 1, which of the following is GREATEST?

 (A) $x - y$

 (B) $\dfrac{x-y}{2}$

 (C) $\dfrac{1}{x}$

 (D) $\dfrac{1}{y}$

 (E) $y - x$

Step 1: Choose our own numbers.

Let's make $x = -1$ and $y = 2$. These are nice round numbers and work with the limits given by the problem.

Step 2: Plug into answer choices and see what gives us the GREATEST number.

 (A) $x - y = -1 - 2 = -3$

 (B) $\dfrac{x-y}{2} = \dfrac{-1-2}{2} = -\dfrac{3}{2}$

 (C) $\dfrac{1}{x} = \dfrac{1}{-1} = -1$

 (D) $\dfrac{1}{y} = \dfrac{1}{2}$

 (E) $y - x = 2 - (-1) = 2 + 1 = 3$

By plugging in our own numbers, we can clearly see that choice E gives us the GREATEST number, so we choose choice E and get it right!

One thing to note about the strategy of plugging in is that you can use it even when a question asks what must be true or what is always true. Just keep plugging different numbers into the answer choices until you have ruled out all but one answer choice.

Strategy #3: If a question asks for the value of a variable, plug in answer choices

For this strategy, keep in mind that a variable is not always a letter. The problem might define x as the number of cars, or it might just ask you what the number of cars is. Either way, it is still asking for the value of a variable and you can use this strategy.

Here is how you use this strategy:

Step 1: Put your answer choices in order from least to greatest if they are not already in that order.

Step 2: Plug the middle answer choice into the problem to see if it works.

Step 3: If the middle choice does not work, go bigger or smaller depending on what you got for the middle answer choice.

Here is an example:

1. A fence is going to be built around a cow pasture. The width of the fenced-in area is to be half the length of the fenced-in area. If the farmer uses exactly 24 yards of fencing, what is the width of the fenced-in area?
   - (A) 1 yard
   - (B) 2 yards
   - (C) 3 yards
   - (D) 4 yards
   - (E) 8 yards

In this case, the answer choices are already in order (they usually are), so we can skip step 1 and go right to step 2.

Step 2: Plug in middle answer choice.

In this case, we make the width equal to 3 in order to test out answer choice C. If the width is 3 yards, then the length must be 6 yards. If we add 2 widths and 2 lengths, then we get a perimeter of 18 yards. The problem tells us that the distance around is 24, however, so we know that choice C does not work. Not only do we know that choice C does not work, but we also know that we need a longer width in order to get a perimeter of 24 yards.

Step 3: Go bigger or smaller if the middle answer choice did not work

Next, we make the width 4 yards in order to test out choice D. If the width is 4 yards, then the length must be 8 yards. If we add 2 widths and 2 lengths to get the perimeter, then the perimeter in this case is 24 yards. That is exactly the distance around that the problem gave us, so we know that choice D is correct.

Strategy #4: If you can, find a range that the answer should fall within

Since you are not allowed to use a calculator on this test, try to see if you can figure out two numbers that an answer should fall in between.

Here is an example:

1. $90 - 6\frac{7}{18} =$

   (A) $82\frac{11}{18}$

   (B) $83\frac{11}{18}$

   (C) $84\frac{7}{18}$

   (D) $84\frac{11}{18}$

   (E) $85\frac{11}{18}$

To solve this problem, we could do a lot of math. Or we could figure out what numbers the answer should fall in between and then use the fact that this is a multiple-choice test to our advantage.

The number $6\frac{7}{18}$ falls in between 6 and 7. $90 - 6 = 84$ and $90 - 7 = 83$. That tells us that our answer should fall in between 83 and 84. Only answer choice B does, so that is the correct answer.

Those are the basics that you need to know for the math section. As you go through the workouts, you will learn content and the strategies that work for specific problem types.

Workouts

Now that you have the strategies, it is time to head to the workouts!

The format of each workout is very predictable so that you can focus on the material and not the directions. Here is what you should look for:

- Vocabulary
  - Each vocabulary section introduces roots and words with those roots. Memorize these roots because there will be different words in later workouts with those same roots. Workouts #6 and #12 include reviews of the roots previously introduced.
  - Each vocabulary section also has a word to remember. These are words that you just need to memorize.
- Practice for the verbal section
  - At first, the focus will be more on strategy than content. Be patient and work through it. We want the strategy to become automatic so that you don't even have to think about it on test day. Think of this part as being like soccer drills. Not always fun, but totally necessary for game day.
- Practice for the reading section
  - We will start out with working on identifying specific and general questions, then there will be one reading passage followed by questions in each workout.
- Practice for the math sections
  - The focus here is to get through as much of the content as possible. Be sure to understand why you missed questions before moving on to the next workout.

You may notice that, in Workouts #2 and #3, there are blanks in the strategy summaries for you to fill in. Please do NOT skip these sections. The goal of this book is to make success automatic, so we have to practice. Gradually, the workouts will transition from telling you all of the strategies beforehand to having you complete a checklist after you are done.

There is a method to this madness. The repetition will make the strategies stick even when there is stress on test day.

Also, make flashcards for words that you do not know and practice them frequently! Seriously, take them in the car, to study hall, and everywhere else that you go.

Go get 'em!

Vocabulary

Roots

Below are some roots. I will give you the definition of each root and then two examples of words that have that root. Look up the meanings of those words and write the definitions in the blanks provided. As you look up the definition of each word, think about how it relates to the root. After you write the definition of each word, write a sentence using the word or a memory trick or association for remembering the word.

Root: *de*
Definition – the opposite of or away from
Examples:
Deter
Definition:
Sentence or memory trick:
Descent
Definition:
Sentence or memory trick:

Root: *cis*
Definition – to cut
Examples:
Excise
Definition:
Sentence or memory trick:
Concise
Definition:
Sentence or memory trick:

Word to remember!

Frugal – adjective describing someone who doesn't like to spend money
Example: My mother says she is frugal, but I say she is cheap!

Now, MAKE FLASHCARDS FOR ALL THE WORDS ABOVE – AND STUDY THEM!

Verbal section

Synonyms strategies

If you know the word, think of a definition before you look at answer choices.

If you have heard the word but can't define it:

1. Use context – in what sentence or phrase have you heard the word before?
2. Positive or negative – write a plus or minus sign next to the question word, rule out answer choices that are opposite or neutral.
3. Look for roots and word parts – ask yourself what other words this word looks like.

Synonyms practice

Before you circle the answer, write the strategy you used from above beside the question word.

1. INCISION: *Strategy:*
   - (A) smile
   - (B) mockery
   - (C) accident
   - (D) cut
   - (E) excuse

2. THRIFTY: *Strategy:*
   - (A) swift
   - (B) frugal
   - (C) mean
   - (D) stubborn
   - (E) frumpy

3. DETOUR: *Strategy:*
    (A) roundabout path
    (B) needle
    (C) fulcrum
    (D) center
    (E) road

Analogies strategies

Our basic strategies for analogies are:

1. If you know the question words, make a sentence from them.

2. If you don't know the question words, go to the answer choices and:
    (A) Try to make a sentence with the answer choices. Rule out any that do not have a strong relationship. If you hear yourself using the words "can", "maybe", "could", or "sometimes", you are talking yourself into the wrong answer.
    (B) With the choices left, try to plug the question words into the sentence that you made with the answer choice words. Could it work?

3. If you are stuck on any of the last ten analogies, pick the answer choice with the weirdest word.

Analogies practice

Listed below are some of the common relationships used on this test:

1. Occupation – one word is the job of the other word

2. Part of – one word is a part of the other word

3. Type of – one word is a type of the other word, which is a broader category

4. Used for – one word is used to do the other word

5. Degree – the words have roughly the same meaning, only one is more extreme

6. Characteristic of – one word is a characteristic of the other

7. Synonyms – the words are synonyms

8. Antonyms – the words are opposite in meaning

9. Found in – one word is found in the other

10. Grammatical – one word has a grammatical relationship to the other

Below are sample analogies. For each one, write the number of the relationship from the previous page that it uses.

1. Baker is to bread as   *Relationship #____*
2. Elbow is arm as   *Relationship #____*
3. Scythe is to cut as   *Relationship #____*
4. Miffed is to irate as   *Relationship #____*
5. Frugal is to cheapskate as   *Relationship #____*
6. Wing is to plane as   *Relationship #____*
7. Concise is to wordy as   *Relationship #____*
8. Convince is to persuade as   *Relationship #____*
9. Snake is to reptile as   *Relationship #____*
10. Monkey is to jungle as   *Relationship #____*

Reading section

Reading strategies

The first step when you approach each passage is to look at the questions. You will want to label each question with either "S" or "G". If it is a specific question, label it with "S". If it is a general question, label it with "G".

Then read the passage. Answer specific questions as you go. Answer general questions at the end.

Secrets for answering specific questions:

1. You can almost always underline the correct answer in the passage for these questions. If you can't underline your answer (often restated using synonyms), then you haven't found the right answer – keep looking!
2. The wrong answer choices often take the same words from the passage and then twist around the order so that they have a different meaning.
3. Look out for assumptions that you make that are not backed up by the passage.

Secrets for general questions:

1. They often have the words "mainly" or "primarily" in them.
2. Before answering these questions, reread the last sentence of the entire passage.
3. The wrong answers are often mentioned in the passage, but they are details and NOT the main idea.

Reading practice

Label the following with "G" or "S": ("G" is for general, "S" is for specific)

1. This passage is primarily about
2. According to the passage, all of the following are rituals of the Navajo EXCEPT
3. The purpose of this document was to
4. The passage implies that the secession of Southern states happened in the year
5. In this poem, the path represents which of the following

Math section

Math strategies

Our general strategies include:

1. Estimate – this is a multiple choice test!
2. If there are variables in the answer choices, try plugging in your own numbers. If it is a "must be true" question, try plugging in weird numbers such as negatives, zero, and fractions.
3. If they ask for the value of a variable, plug in answer choices.
4. If you can, find a range that the answer should fall within.

Math practice

1. There are 25 students in a class. 18 of these students play the piano. 9 of these students play the trombone. How many students must play both the piano and the trombone?

   (A) 1
   (B) 2
   (C) 3
   (D) 9
   (E) 25

Questions 2-3 refer to the following definition.

For all real numbers q and r, $q \# r = (q + r) \times (q - r)$

Example: $2 \# 3 = (2 + 3) \times (2 - 3) = 5 \times (-1) = -5$

2. $5 \# 4 =$

   (A) 6
   (B) 7
   (C) 8
   (D) 9
   (E) 10

3. If $T \# 2 = 77$, then $T =$

   (A) 3
   (B) 5
   (C) 9
   (D) 11
   (E) 20

4. Sarah has y baseball cards. She has seven more cards than Tim. Tim has four fewer cards than Sheila. In terms of y, how many baseball cards does Sheila have?

   (A) $y - 3$
   (B) $y - 7$
   (C) $y - 10$
   (D) $y + 4$
   (E) $y + 10$

5. John is laying a brick patio. His bricks are 3 inches by 4 inches. The patio he wants to create will be 5 feet by 5 feet. How many bricks will he need?

   (A) 12
   (B) 25
   (C) 60
   (D) 150
   (E) 300

6. What is the ratio of 3 ft. 4 in. to 5 ft.?

   (A) 1 to 3
   (B) 1 to 2
   (C) 2 to 3
   (D) 2 to 4
   (E) 3 to 5

7. If $x = 3$ and $y = 5$, then what is the value of $2xy^2$?

   (A) 30
   (B) 45
   (C) 90
   (D) 150
   (E) 900

Workout #1 Answers

Vocabulary

I am not giving you answers for the definitions – look them up!

Verbal section

Synonyms practice

1. D – The word "incision" has the "cis" root, which means to cut.

2. B – Thrifty and frugal are two words that you have to memorize. Be sure to make flashcards if you missed this one.

3. A – "De" means opposite or away from. A detour takes you away from something, so it is a roundabout path. Don't be fooled by choice E. Detours are often on roads, but detour and road don't mean the same thing.

Analogies practice

1. #1 – A baker's job is to make bread.

2. #2 or #4 – An elbow is part of the arm, and an elbow is used to bend the arm. You would have to go through the answer choices to see which relationship they were looking for.

3. #4 – A scythe is used to cut.

4. #5 – Miffed is a little angry, irate is really, really angry.

5. #6 – Frugal is a characteristic of a cheapskate.

6. #2 – A wing is part of a plane.

7. #8 – Concise and wordy have opposite meanings.

8. #7 – Convince and persuade have the same meaning.

9. #3 – A snake is a type of reptile.

10. #9 – A monkey is found in the jungle.

Reading section

Reading practice

1. G – The word "primarily" tells us that it is general.

2. S – This is looking for details.

3. G – The question is referring to the document as a whole so it is general.

4. S – Questions with the word "implies" are almost always specific on the SSAT.

5. S or G – It is probably specific, but it is possible that the whole poem was about the path. Remember, we don't obsess over being exact when we label questions "S" or "G". Sometimes we just have to go with it and see how the passage plays out.

Math section

Math practice

1. B – If we add $18 + 9$, then we get 27. However, there are only 25 students. This tells us that there must be an overlap of 2 students who play both instruments.

2. D – Don't worry if you were confused about what the # sign meant. You aren't supposed to know. This is a particular type of SSAT question that defines a function for you and then you have to plug in. For this question, the 5 comes before the # sign, so we plug in 5 for q in the equation. The 4 comes after the # sign, so we plug in the 4 for the r in the equation.

   We get:
   $$(5 + 4) \times (5 - 4) = 9 \times 1 = 9$$

3. C – We use the same equation as we did for question 2. Only this time we have to plug in a variable.

   If we plug in, we get:
   $$(T + 2) \times (T - 2) = 77$$

   We could solve the math way, but that could get tricky and we might make a mistake. It would be better just to plug in the answer choices for T and see what works. If we try choice C, we get:
   $$(9 + 2) \times (9 - 2) = 11 \times 7 = 77$$

   Since we get 77 for our answer, choice C is correct.

4. A – We have variables in the answer choices, so we plug in our own numbers. Let's make $y = 10$, so Sarah has 10 baseball cards. She has seven more than Tim, so Tim must have 3 cards. Tim has four fewer cards than Sheila, so Sheila must have 7 cards. We circle 7 since we are looking for how many cards Sheila has. Now we plug in 10 for y in the answer choices and see which gives us 7.

    (A) $y - 3 = 10 - 3 = 7$
    (B) $y - 7 = 10 - 7 = 3$
    (C) $y - 10 = 10 - 10 = 0$
    (D) $y + 4 = 10 + 4 = 14$
    (E) $y + 10 = 10 + 10 = 20$

    Since we get 7 for choice A, and 7 is our target, choice A is the correct answer.

5. E – The first thing that you should notice is that there are both inches and feet as units of measurement in this problem. We need to make sure not to get tripped up by that. The first step is to convert all of the measurements into inches. In order to do that, we multiply 5 feet by 12 to get 60 inches. That tells us that the patio is going to be 60 inches by 60 inches. Let's assume that he lays all the bricks going the same direction. If we divide 60 by 3 (since one side of each brick is 3 inches), we get that he can fit 20 bricks on one side. To see how many bricks fit in the other dimension, we divide 60 by 4 (since the other side of each brick is 4 inches) and get 15. That tells us that the patio will be 20 bricks by 15 bricks, or 20 rows of 15 bricks each. If we multiply 15 times 20, we get that he needs a total of 300 bricks, or answer choice E.

6. C – The key to this question is that we have to put both lengths into the same units. It is easiest to put them both into inches. If we convert 3 ft. 4 in. to inches, we get 40 inches for the first measurement. Now we have to convert 5 feet into inches and we get 60 inches for the second length. Now our ratio is 40 to 60. We aren't done yet, though, since we can reduce that ratio just like we would reduce a fraction. If we divide both 40 and 60 by 20, we get a ratio of 2 to 3, or answer choice C.

7. D – This problem is pretty straightforward. We just have to plug in 3 for x and 5 for y in the expression given. This gives us $2(3)(5)^2 = 150$.

Workout #2

Vocabulary

Roots

Below are some roots. I will give you the definition of each root and then two examples of words that have that root. Look up the meanings of those words and write the definitions in the blanks provided. As you look up the definition of each word, think about how it relates to the root. After you write the definition of each word, write a sentence using the word or a memory trick or association for remembering the word.

Root: *fid*
Definition – trust or faith
Examples:
Fidelity
Definition:
Sentence or memory trick:
Infidel
Definition:
Sentence or memory trick:

Root: *pan*
Definition – all
Examples:
Panorama
Definition:
Sentence or memory trick:
Panacea
Definition:
Sentence or memory trick:

Word to remember!

Congeal – to thicken or become a solid from a liquid

Example: It is nasty how the fat from French fries congeals when they get cold.

Now, MAKE FLASHCARDS FOR ALL THE WORDS ABOVE – AND STUDY THEM!

Verbal section

Synonyms strategy review

Fill in the blanks:

If you know the word, think of a definition before you look at answer choices.

If you have heard the word but can't define it:

1. Use context – (1)_____?
2. Positive or negative – write a (2)_____ next to the question word, rule out answer choices that are opposite or (3)_____.
3. Look for roots and word parts – (4)_____.

Synonyms practice

Before you circle the answer, write the strategy you used from above beside the question word.

1. DECELERATE: *Strategy:*
   (A) speed up
   (B) turn around
   (C) fall
   (D) stumble
   (E) slow down

2. CONGEAL: *Strategy:*
   (A) smell
   (B) let loose
   (C) curdle
   (D) resist
   (E) rise

3. TREACHERY: *Strategy:*

   (A) event
   (B) perfidy
   (C) salvation
   (D) eulogy
   (E) crowd

Analogies strategy review

Fill in the blanks:

1. If you know the question words, (1)_____.
2. If you don't know the question words, (2)_____ and:
   (A) Try to make a sentence with the answer choices. Rule out any that do not have a strong relationship. If you hear yourself using the words (3)_____ _____, you are talking yourself into the wrong answer.
   (B) With the choices left, (4)_____ into the sentence that you made with the answer choice words. Could it work?
3. If you are stuck on any of the last ten analogies, simply pick the answer choice with the (5)_____.

Analogies practice

Listed below are some of the common relationships used on this test:

1. Occupation – one word is the job of the other word
2. Part of – one word is a part of the other word
3. Type of – one word is a type of the other word, which is a broader category
4. Used for – one word is used to do the other word
5. Degree – the words have roughly the same meaning, only one is more extreme
6. Characteristic of – one word is a characteristic of the other
7. Synonyms – the words are synonyms
8. Antonyms – the words are opposite in meaning
9. Found in – one word is found in the other
10. Grammatical – one word has a grammatical relationship to the other

Below are sample analogies. Write the number of the relationship from the previous page that they use.

1. Policeman is to law enforcement as   *Relationship #___*
2. Magnanimous is to malevolent as   *Relationship #___*
3. Buckle is to belt as   *Relationship #___*
4. Pencil is to writing as   *Relationship #___*
5. Can is to will as   *Relationship #___*
6. Poverty is to wealth as   *Relationship #___*
7. Compass is to navigation as   *Relationship #___*
8. Rivulet is to river as   *Relationship #___*
9. Diamond is to mine as   *Relationship #___*
10. Nimble is to gymnast as   *Relationship #___*

Reading section

Reading strategy review

Fill in the blanks:

The first step when you approach each passage is to (1)_____. You will want to label each question with either (2)_____. If it is a specific question, label it with (3)_____. If it is a general question, label it with (4)_____.

Then read the passage. Answer (5)_____ questions as you go. Answer (6)_____ questions at the end.

Secrets for answering specific questions:

1. You can almost always underline the correct answer in the passage for these questions. If you can't (7)_____ your answer (often restated using synonyms), then (8)_____ – keep looking!
2. The wrong answer choices often take the same words from the passage and then (9)_____.
3. Look out for assumptions that you make that are not (10)_____.

Secrets for general questions:

1. They often have the words (11)_____ in them.
2. Before answering these questions, reread the (12)_____ of the entire passage.
3. The wrong answers are often mentioned in the passage, but they (13)_____.

Reading practice

Label the following with "G" or "S": ("G" is for general, "S" is for specific)

1. An appropriate title for this poem would be
2. According to this passage, Johnny Appleseed
3. The author implies that suffragettes
4. The author's attitude toward early veterinarians can best be described as
5. The author uses the analogy of willows to illustrate that Native Americans

Math section

Math strategy review

Fill in the blanks:

Our general strategies include:

1. _____ – this is a multiple choice test!
2. If there are variables in the answer choices, try _____. If it is a "must be true" question, try plugging in weird numbers such as negatives, zero, and fractions.
3. If they ask for the value of a variable, _____.
4. If you can, _____ that the answer should fall within.

Math practice

1. The glee club was having a flower sale. At 10 AM, they needed to sell five more flowers to reach their goal. By 1 PM, they had exceeded their goal by 12 flowers. How many flowers did they sell between 10 AM and 1 PM?

   (A) 5
   (B) 7
   (C) 10
   (D) 15
   (E) 17

2. If $\frac{1}{3}Q = 9$, then $\frac{2}{3}Q =$

   (A) 3
   (B) 9
   (C) 12
   (D) 18
   (E) 27

3. When two triangular regions overlap, which of the following shapes could describe the overlapping portion?

   I.   Triangle
   II. Square
   III. Rectangle

   (A) I only
   (B) II only
   (C) I and III only
   (D) I, II, and III
   (E) None of the above

4. 25% of $11.95 is closest to which of the following?

   (A) $3.00
   (B) $4.00
   (C) $6.00
   (D) $8.00
   (E) $12.00

5. If the average of 5 consecutive odd numbers is 13, what is the smallest number?

(A) 7
(B) 9
(C) 11
(D) 13
(E) 17

6. Simplify: $(3x^3 + 2x - 4) - (2x^2 - 3x + 9)$

(A) $3x^3 - 2x^2 + 5x - 13$
(B) $3x^3 + 5$
(C) $3x^3 - 4x^2 + 2x + 5$
(D) $x^3 - 2x^2 + x - 13$
(E) $x^3 - 2x^2 + x + 5$

7. $\left(-\dfrac{3}{5}\right)^3 =$

(A) $-\dfrac{9}{25}$

(B) $-\dfrac{27}{125}$

(C) $-\dfrac{3}{5}$

(D) $\dfrac{27}{125}$

(E) $\dfrac{9}{25}$

Workout #2 Answers

Vocabulary

Look them up!

Verbal section

Synonyms strategy review

1. …in what sentence or phrase have you heard the word before
2. …plus or minus sign
3. …neutral
4. …ask yourself what other words this word looks like

Synonyms practice

1. E – The "de" root means opposite. Since accelerate means to speed up, this means that decelerate means the opposite, or to slow down.
2. C – This is a word to remember from this workout. Make sure you create a flashcard if you missed this one!
3. B – Treachery is an act of betrayal. Perfidy has the "fid" root that means faithful. Perfidy means a betrayal of trust, so it is the correct answer. If nothing else, you could have ruled out some choices and then guessed (by the way, a eulogy is a speech of praise).

Analogies strategy review

1. …make a sentence from them
2. …go to the answer choices
3. …can, maybe, could, or sometimes
4. …try to plug the question words
5. …weirdest word

Analogies practice

1. #1 – The job of a policeman is law enforcement.
2. #8 – Magnanimous is generous and giving, malevolent is wishing evil to others.
3. #2 or #4 – A buckle is part of a belt or a buckle is used to close a belt.
4. #4 – A pencil is used for writing.
5. #10 – Can means that something is possible and will means that an action is definite.
6. #8 – Poverty is the opposite of wealth.
7. #4 – A compass is used for navigation.
8. #5 – A rivulet is a really little river.
9. #9 – A diamond is found in a mine.
10. #6 – Nimble is a characteristic of a gymnast.

Reading section

Reading strategy review

1. …look at the questions
2. …S or G
3. …S
4. …G
5. …specific
6. …general
7. …underline
8. …you haven't found the right answer
9. …twist around the order so that they have a different meaning
10. …backed up by the passage
11. …mainly or primarily
12. …last sentence
13. …are details and NOT the main idea

Reading practice

1. G – A title has to sum up the passage as a whole, so it is a general question.

2. S – Even though it looks general, "according to the passage" questions are almost always looking for a detail on the SSAT.

3. S – Because we know how the SSAT generally works, we know that "implies" questions are usually looking for a detail.

4. S or G – It depends on whether or not the whole passage is about early veterinarians. I would guess that the question is specific since it uses the qualifier "early". You would have to make sure you chose the answer that summed up the author's attitude about "early veterinarians" and not just veterinarians in general.

5. S – An analogy is usually a small part of a passage and not the entire thing.

Math section

Math strategy review

1. Estimate
2. …plugging in your own numbers
3. …plug in answer choices
4. …find a range

Math practice

1. E – To solve this problem, let's plug in our own number for their goal. Let's say they wanted to sell 10 flowers. So at 10 AM they would have sold 5 less than their goal, or 5 flowers. By 1 PM, they would have sold 12 more than their goal, or 22 flowers. If we find the difference between these two numbers, we get that they sold $22 - 5 = 17$ flowers in between.

2. D – $\frac{2}{3}$ is twice as much as $\frac{1}{3}$. That means that the value of $\frac{2}{3}Q$ should be twice the value of $\frac{1}{3}Q$. Twice the value of 9 is 18, so choice D is our answer.

3. D – Draw this one out. If one tip of one triangle overlaps with one side of the other, a triangle will be created. If one tip of one triangle overlaps with a tip of the other, a quadrilateral will be created. Since the question doesn't tell us that the triangles can't be right triangles, we have to assume that is a possibility. If we have two right triangles and the right angles overlap, then we could create both a square and a rectangle. Therefore, I, II, and III all work.

4. A – We can round off since the question uses the words "closest to". $11.95 is about $12.00, so we can use that number for calculations. Now we can use the trick of finding 10% and then use that to find 25%. To get 10%, we can just move the decimal point one place to the left, so we get $1.20 is 10% of $12.00.

   Here is how we figure out 25% from that:

   $$10\% = 1.20$$
   $$10\% = 1.20$$
   $$+5\% = 0.60$$
   $$\text{-----------------}$$
   $$25\% = 3.00$$

5. B – The trick to this problem is remembering that it is consecutive ODD numbers and that they are looking for the SMALLEST number. I would circle these two facts in the problem because they are easy to forget. If the numbers are consecutive, then the average is also the middle number. That means there must be two numbers before 13, so we can count backwards by two. If the third number is 13, then the second number must be 11, so the first number must be 9. The smallest number is 9, so choice B is correct.

6. A – The first step here is to rewrite the expression without the parentheses. The important thing to remember is to distribute the negative sign to all of the elements in the second set of parentheses:

   $$(3x^3 + 2x - 4) - (2x^2 - 3x + 9) = 3x^3 + 2x - 4 - 2x^2 + 3x - 9$$

   Now we combine like terms to get $3x^3 - 2x^2 + 5x - 13$, so choice A is correct.

7. B – To answer this question, we have to remember that if there is an exponent for a fraction in parentheses then we have to apply that exponent to both the numerator and denominator. Also, we need to remember that since the number in the parentheses is negative and the exponent is odd, the final answer will be negative. The math looks like this:

   $$\left(-\frac{3}{5}\right)^3 = -\frac{3^3}{5^3} = -\frac{3 \times 3 \times 3}{5 \times 5 \times 5} = -\frac{27}{125}$$

Vocabulary

Roots

Below are some roots. I will give you the definition of each root and then two examples of words that have that root. Look up the meanings of those words and write the definitions in the blanks provided. As you look up the definition of each word, think about how it relates to the root. After you write the definition of each word, write a sentence using the word or a memory trick or association for remembering the word.

Root: *loc / loq / log*
Definition – to speak
Examples:
Eloquent
Definition:
Sentence or memory trick:
Neologism
Definition:
Sentence or memory trick:

Root: *magna*
Definition – big
Examples:
Magnanimous
Definition:
Sentence or memory trick:
Magnificent
Definition:
Sentence or memory trick:

Word to remember!

Tact – words or actions designed not to offend another person (A person with tact is tactful.)
Example: You have to show a certain amount of tact when telling someone he has a booger on his face.

Now, MAKE FLASHCARDS FOR ALL THE WORDS ABOVE – AND STUDY THEM!

Verbal section

Synonyms strategy review

Fill in the blanks:

If you know the word, think of a definition before you look at answer choices.

If you have heard the word but can't define it:

1. Use (1)_____ in what sentence or phrase have you heard the word before?

2. (2)_____ – write a plus or minus sign next to the question word, rule out answer choices that are opposite or neutral.

3. (3)_____ – ask yourself what other words this word looks like.

Synonyms practice

Before you circle the answer, write the strategy you used from above beside the question word.

1. LOQUACIOUS: *Strategy:*
   (A) jubilant
   (B) fussy
   (C) fundamental
   (D) profound
   (E) talkative

2. GENEROUS: *Strategy:*

   (A) magnanimous
   (B) funky
   (C) klutzy
   (D) gifted
   (E) slow

3. DERIDE: *Strategy:*

   (A) elevate
   (B) obsess
   (C) ruin
   (D) ridicule
   (E) chase

Analogies strategy review

Fill in the blanks:

1. If (1)_____, make a sentence from them.
2. If (2)_____, go to the answer choices and:
   (A) (3)_____ with the answer choices. Rule out any that do not have a strong relationship. If you hear yourself using the words "can", "maybe", "could", or "sometimes", you are (4)_____.
   (B) (5)_____, try to plug the question words into the sentence that you made with the answer choice words. Could it work?
3. (6)_____, simply pick the answer choice with the weirdest word.

Analogies practice

Now that you are more familiar with the relationships, pretend the following are answer choices when you don't know the question words. Rule out the ones that are not related. Remember, if you use "can", "maybe", "could", or "sometimes", it is not a strong relationship!

1. clown is to tiger

2. shoe is to foot

3. sour is to sweet

4. perimeter is to circle

5. frugal is to spendthrift

6. corral is to horses

7. morning is to tired

8. overcast is to sunshine

Reading section

Reading strategy review

Fill in the blanks:

The first step when you approach each passage is to (1)_____.
You will want to label each question with either "S" or "G". If it is a (2)_____
question, label it with "S". If it is a (3)_____ question, label it with "G".

Then read the passage. Answer (4)_____ questions as you go.
Answer (5)_____ questions at the end.

Secrets for answering specific questions:

1. You can almost always underline the correct answer in the passage for these
   questions. If you can't underline your answer (often (6)_____),
   then you haven't found the right answer – (7)_____!

2. The wrong answer choices often take the same words from the passage and then
   (8)_____.

3. Look out for assumptions that you make that are not (9)_____
   _____.

Secrets for general questions:

1. They often have the words (10)_____ in them.

2. Before answering these questions, reread the (11)_____ of the entire
   passage.

3. The wrong answers are (12)_____,
   but they are details and NOT the main idea.

Reading practice

Label the following with a "G" or "S": (G is for general, S is for specific)

1. The Battle of Midway was fought
2. Which of the following best expresses the author's main point
3. The passage implies
4. The tone of the passage can best be described as
5. Which of the following statements about exports would the author most likely agree with

Math section

Math strategy review

Fill in the blanks:

Our general strategies include:

1. _____ – this is a multiple choice test!
2. If there are variables in the answer choices, try _____.
   If it is a "must be true" question, try plugging in weird numbers such as negatives, zero, and fractions.
3. If they ask for the value of a variable, _____.
4. If you can, _____ that the answer should fall within.

Math practice

1.

How the Smiths spent their $200 road trip budget

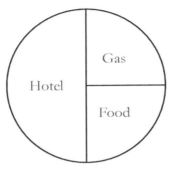

Figure 1

According to the graph in figure 1, how much did the Smith family spend on gas for their road trip?

(A) $25
(B) $50
(C) $75
(D) $100
(E) $150

2. For a bake sale, the track team sold cookies and doughnuts. They sold twice as many cookies as doughnuts. Which of the following could have been the total number of cookies and doughnuts sold?

(A) 10
(B) 14
(C) 16
(D) 21
(E) 25

3. A three-man team competed in a relay race. Each person completed one leg of the race. If the average time per leg was 3 minutes and 35 seconds, what was the total time it took the team to complete the race?

(A) 9 minutes and 35 seconds

(B) 10 minutes and 15 seconds

(C) 10 minutes and 45 seconds

(D) 11 minutes

(E) 11 minutes and 35 seconds

4. Farmer Bill must put up a new fence around his hog pen. He needs the total perimeter to be 12 yards. If the fence comes in segments 2 feet long, how many segments will he need?

(A) 3

(B) 4

(C) 6

(D) 12

(E) 18

5. Five friends each chip in 7 dollars for a present. If two more people chipped in for the same present and the expense was shared equally, how much less would each person have to pay?

(A) $2

(B) $3

(C) $5

(D) $7

(E) $35

6. Find the missing term in the sequence below:

$$\frac{1}{8}, \frac{1}{4}, \frac{3}{8}, \frac{1}{2}, \frac{5}{8}, \underline{}$$

(A) $\frac{1}{2}$

(B) $\frac{5}{7}$

(C) $\frac{6}{9}$

(D) $\frac{3}{4}$

(E) $\frac{7}{8}$

7. Which number is equivalent to four thousand one hundred three and twenty-seven hundredths?

(A) 4,103.027

(B) 4,103.27

(C) 4,127.003

(D) 4,127.027

(E) 4,127.27

Workout #3 Answers

Vocabulary

Look them up!

Verbal section

Synonyms strategy review

1. …context
2. Positive or negative
3. Look for roots and word parts

Synonyms practice

1. E – Loquacious has the "loq" root, which means to speak. A loquacious person is talkative.
2. A – "Magna" means big, and the "anim" root means spirit, so if you are magnanimous you have a big spirit, or are generous.
3. D – "De" is a negative root, so we know the answer must be negative. Ruin and ridicule are both negative. However, do you notice that deride and ridicule both have "rid" in them? To deride someone is to ridicule (or criticize) him.

Analogies strategy review

1. …you know the question words
2. …you don't know the question words
3. Try to make a sentence
4. …talking yourself into the wrong answer
5. With the choices left
6. If you are stuck on any of the last ten analogies

Analogies practice

The following are NOT related: 1, 4, 7

For #1, a clown and a tiger might both be in the circus, but that is not a strong relationship. Remember that on this test, belonging to the same broader category (circus performers) doesn't count as a relationship.

For #4, it is tempting to say they are related because they are both geometry terms. However, a circle has a circumference, not a perimeter.

For #7, you could be tired in the morning, but you might not be tired at all. If you have to use the word "could", the relationship is not strong enough.

Reading section

Reading strategies

1. …look at the questions
2. …specific
3. …general
4. …specific
5. …general
6. …restated using synonyms
7. …keep looking
8. …twist around the order so that they have a different meaning
9. …backed up by the passage
10. …primarily or mainly
11. …last sentence
12. …often mentioned in the passage

Reading practice

1. S – This question is asking about a specific detail.

2. G – The words "main point" let us know it is a general question.

3. S – Even though it looks general, a question with the word "implies" is almost always looking for a detail.

4. G – This question is asking about the tone of the entire passage.

5. S – These questions generally are not about the main idea, but rather a detail.

Math section

Math strategy review

1. Estimate

2. …plugging in your own numbers

3. …plug in answer choices

4. …find a range

Math practice

1. B – The Smiths spent about a quarter of their budget on gas. Their total budget was $200, and if we divide $200 into four pieces, or quarters, then we get $50 spent on gas.

2. D – The ratio of cookies to doughnuts was 2 to 1. If we convert these ratios into fractions, we get that $\frac{1}{3}$ of their sales were doughnuts and $\frac{2}{3}$ were cookies. This tells us that the total number of items sold must be divisible by 3. Answer choice D is the only one divisible by 3.

3. C – If we rearrange the average equation, we get that average × number of numbers = total. This tells us that we should multiply 3 minutes and 35 seconds by three. This gives us a total of 10 minutes and 45 seconds.

4. E – We have both feet and yards in this problem. Our first step is to convert the yards into feet. To do this, we multiply 12 yards times 3 feet per yard to get 36 feet around the hog pen. We can then divide this number by 2 since each segment is 2 feet long. We get that the farmer will need 36 ÷ 2 = 18 segments.

5. A – If we multiply 5 × 7, that tells us that $35 was collected originally. If two more people gave money, then there are now seven people giving money. Since the total amount of money collected did not change, we divide $35 by 7 to get that each person now gives $5. This is $2 less than the original $7 a piece, so choice A is correct.

6. D – The key to answering this question is to figure out what we add to get from one number to the next. In order to do that, we have to have a common denominator. If we convert each fraction so that it has a denominator of 8, we get:

$$\frac{1}{8}, \frac{1}{4}, \frac{3}{8}, \frac{1}{2}, \frac{5}{8}, \text{---} = \frac{1}{8}, \frac{2}{8}, \frac{3}{8}, \frac{4}{8}, \frac{5}{8}, \text{---}$$

This makes it clear that the next term is $\frac{6}{8}$. Now we have to reduce the fraction by dividing the numerator and the denominator by 2 to get $\frac{3}{4}$.

7. B – The key to this question is to get all of the place values straight and remember that the word "and" indicates a decimal point. If we use ruling out, we can start with what comes after the word "and". Since the first place to the right of the decimal is tenths and the second is hundredths, we know that our number should end in .27. This allows us to rule out A, C, and D. We also know there needs to be a three in the number, so we can rule out choice E. This leaves us with choice B.

Workout #4

Vocabulary

Roots

Below are some roots. I will give you the definition of each root and then two examples of words that have that root. Look up the meanings of those words and write the definitions in the blanks provided. As you look up the definition of each word, think about how it relates to the root. After you write the definition of each word, write a sentence using the word or a memory trick or association for remembering the word.

Root: *bene*
   Definition – good or well
Examples:
   Beneficient
      Definition:
      Sentence or memory trick:
   Benefactor
      Definition:
      Sentence or memory trick:

Root: *chron*
   Definition – time
Examples:
   Chronic
      Definition:
      Sentence or memory trick:
   Anachronism
      Definition:
      Sentence or memory trick:

Word to remember!

Scull – a boat used for rowing
Example: In the fall, you can often see sculls cruising along the Charles River.

Now, MAKE FLASHCARDS FOR ALL THE WORDS ABOVE – AND STUDY THEM!

Verbal section

Synonyms strategies

If you know the word, think of a definition before you look at answer choices.

If you have heard the word but can't define it:

1. Use context – in what sentence or phrase have you heard the word before?
2. Positive or negative – write a plus or minus sign next to the question word, rule out answer choices that are opposite or neutral.
3. Look for roots and word parts – ask yourself what other words this word looks like.

Synonyms practice

Before you circle the answer, write the strategy you used from above beside the question word.
TIME YOURSELF – THESE QUESTIONS SHOULD TAKE LESS THAN 3 MINUTES.

1. BENEDICTION: *Strategy:*
   (A) meeting
   (B) accident
   (C) ruse
   (D) blessing
   (E) race

2. RECURRING: *Strategy:*

   (A) last
   (B) chronic
   (C) symbolic
   (D) rusty
   (E) fast paced

3. DEVALUE: *Strategy:*

   (A) debase
   (B) increase
   (C) end
   (D) meditate
   (E) guess

4. LOQUACIOUS: *Strategy:*

   (A) mundane
   (B) rowdy
   (C) moist
   (D) extinct
   (E) talkative

5. DIPLOMATIC: *Strategy:*

   (A) rough
   (B) flawed
   (C) tactful
   (D) growing
   (E) sharp

Analogies strategies

1. If you know the question words, make a sentence from them.

2. If you don't know the question words, go to the answer choices and:

   (A) Try to make a sentence with the answer choices. Rule out any that do not have a strong relationship. If you hear yourself using the words "can", "maybe", "could", or "sometimes", you are talking yourself into the wrong answer.

   (B) With the choices left, try to plug the question words into the sentence that you made with the answer choice words. Could it work?

3. If you are stuck on any of the last ten analogies, simply pick the answer choice with the weirdest word.

Analogies practice

Listed below are some of the common relationships used on this test:

1. Occupation – one word is the job of the other word
2. Part of – one word is a part of the other word
3. Type of – one word is a type of the other word, which is a broader category
4. Used for – one word is used to do the other word
5. Degree – the words have roughly the same meaning, only one is more extreme
6. Characteristic of – one word is a characteristic of the other
7. Synonyms – the words are synonyms
8. Antonyms – the words are opposite in meaning
9. Found in – one word is found in the other
10. Grammatical – one word has a grammatical relationship to the other

Below are sample analogy questions.

Next to each question:

(A) If you know the question words, write in the relationship number from the list above.
(B) If you don't know the question words, write in WB (for working backwards, which is what we are doing when we rule out answer choices and then guess.)

TIME YOURSELF – THESE QUESTIONS SHOULD TAKE LESS THAN 3 MINUTES.

1. Panacea is to cure as   *Relationship # / Strategy:*
    (A) vacuum is to clean
    (B) medicine is to infect
    (C) butcher is to carve
    (D) water is to pour
    (E) hindrance is to enjoy

2. Magnificent is to miniscule as   *Relationship # / Strategy:*

   (A) tremendous is to noisy
   (B) superficial is to shallow
   (C) abstract is to concrete
   (D) generous is to benevolent
   (E) fundamental is to worrisome

3. Infidelity is to betrayal as   *Relationship # / Strategy:*

   (A) peace is to riot
   (B) clown is to performer
   (C) hammer is to carpenter
   (D) force is to bravery
   (E) luck is to wealth

4. Excise is to eradicate as   *Relationship # / Strategy:*

   (A) chronicle is to record
   (B) recede is to storm
   (C) ignite is to resist
   (D) write is to listen
   (E) deter is to forbid

5. Have is to had as   *Relationship # / Strategy:*

   (A) might is to may
   (B) are is to were
   (C) was is to is
   (D) be is to end
   (E) call is to listen

Reading section

Reading strategies

The first step when you approach each passage is to look at the questions. You will want to label each question with either "S" or "G". If it is a specific question, label it with "S". If it is a general question, label it with "G".

Then read the passage. Answer specific questions as you go. Answer general questions at the end.

Secrets for answering specific questions:

1. You can almost always underline the correct answer in the passage for specific questions. If you can't underline your answer (often restated using synonyms), then you haven't found the right answer – keep looking!
2. The wrong answer choices often take the same words from the passage and then twist around the order so that they have a different meaning.
3. Look out for assumptions that you make that are not backed up by the passage.

Secrets for general questions:

1. They often have the words "mainly" or "primarily" in them.
2. Before answering these questions, reread the last sentence of the entire passage.
3. The wrong answers are often mentioned in the passage, but they are details and NOT the main idea.

Reading practice

Below is a practice reading passage. It is a science passage, one of the many types that you will see on this test.

TIME YOURSELF – THIS PASSAGE AND QUESTIONS SHOULD TAKE A TOTAL OF 5 MINUTES

If you look into the night sky, you may notice something that looks like a very bright star. It might, in fact, be Venus. The moon is the brightest object in the night sky, but Venus ranks second. Venus is also the second planet from the sun.

Line 5   Venus has been nicknamed Earth's "sister planet" because it is similar to Earth in size, gravity, and composition. It is even believed that at one time, Venus may have possessed oceans, just like those on Earth. However, these oceans evaporated long ago leaving just a dry and dusty surface covered with volcanoes.

Volcanoes are one of the most prominent features of Venus' geography.
10   There is a large amount of sulfur in Venus' atmosphere, which indicates that these volcanoes have been active some time in recent history. However, there is no evidence of lava, which leaves scientists puzzled. Volcanoes or volcanic activity caused many of the surface features on Venus.

Venus has long fascinated people in many cultures. It is often called either
15   the "morning star" or the "evening star". Depending upon where Earth and Venus are in their relative rotations around the sun, it can appear to either be the last star on the horizon in the morning or the first star in evening. Pythagoras is often given credit for discovering that these two stars were actually the same body some time in the sixth century, B.C. We now know, of course, that these are not stars at all,
20   but rather the planet Venus.

Venus remained relatively unknown until the twentieth century. After a few unfruitful attempts, in 1966 the unmanned probe Venera 3 crashed into the surface of Venus. Unfortunately, its equipment was damaged and it was unable to send information back to Earth. The Venera 4, however, was able to safely land on
25   Venus and communicate data back to scientists. Since then, other probes have provided us with further information about Earth's "sister planet".

1. The author states that Venus has been called Earth's "sister planet" (line 5) because

   (A) it is believed that Venus spun off of Earth
   (B) it is similar in color to Earth
   (C) it has oceans like Earth does
   (D) early scientists thought that it rotated around Earth
   (E) it is about the same size as Earth and made up of a similar composition

2. Which of the following can currently be found on Venus?

   (A) oceans
   (B) lava
   (C) volcanoes
   (D) grass
   (E) evidence of human life

3. According to the passage, who first identified that the "morning star" and the "evening star" were in fact the same celestial body?

   (A) Pythagoras
   (B) modern scientists
   (C) Venera 3
   (D) Venera 4
   (E) none of the above

4. The author's main purpose for writing this passage is to

   (A) explain the mystery of why Venus has volcanoes but no lava
   (B) give a detailed history of planetary research
   (C) explain the origin of Venus' name
   (D) provide general information about Venus
   (E) compare Venus to Earth

5. According to the passage, all of the following are true about Venus EXCEPT

   (A) the first unmanned vehicle to make it to Venus was Venera 3
   (B) Venus is actually a star
   (C) Venus is the second planet from the sun
   (D) Venus is Earth's "sister planet"
   (E) the "morning star" and the "evening star" are actually both Venus

Math section

Math practice

TIME YOURSELF – THESE PROBLEMS SHOULD TAKE YOU ABOUT 9 MINUTES TOTAL

1. If $T + 25 = 28$, then $T \times 25 =$

   (A) $\dfrac{3}{25}$

   (B) 1

   (C) 3

   (D) 75

   (E) 76

2. A piece of string 3 feet long can be cut into how many 4 inch pieces?

   (A) 6

   (B) 8

   (C) 9

   (D) 12

   (E) 15

3. 712970

   A   B

   The value of the "7" in the A place above is how many times the value of the "7" in the B place above?

   (A) 10,000

   (B) 1,000

   (C) 100

   (D) 10

   (E) 1

4. In the figure above, if 3 lines meet as shown, what is the value of x?

    (A) 15
    (B) 20
    (C) 30
    (D) 40
    (E) 90

5. If $a + b$ is divisible by 5, which of the following is also divisible by 5?

    (A) $a \times b$
    (B) $5 + (a \times b)$
    (C) $5a + 2b$
    (D) $(a + b) \div 5$
    (E) $(3 \times a) + (3 \times b)$

6. Evaluate: $40 - 2(3) + 24 \div 6$

    (A) 10
    (B) 23
    (C) 38
    (D) 118
    (E) 120

7. A deck of cards is labeled 1-60. If a card is randomly selected, what is the probability that the number on it will be divisible by both 3 and 5?

    (A) $\dfrac{1}{60}$

    (B) $\dfrac{1}{20}$

    (C) $\dfrac{1}{15}$

    (D) $\dfrac{1}{5}$

    (E) $\dfrac{1}{3}$

Workout #4 Answers

Vocabulary

Look them up!

Verbal section

Synonyms practice

1. D – Benediction has the "bene" root that means good and also the "dict" root that means to speak. Literally, benediction means to speak good, but it has come to mean blessing.

2. B – The prefix "re" means again, so recurrent is something that happens again and again. Chronic (the "chron" root means time) has the same meaning.

3. A – The prefix "de" means opposite or away from, so devalue means to take away value. To debase means the same thing. Did you notice that these words have the same prefix?

4. E – The "loq" root means to talk, so loquacious is talkative.

5. C – A diplomat tries not to offend anyone, so diplomatic means tactful. Tact is a word to remember from Workout #3, so make a flashcard if you haven't already.

Analogies practice

1. A, relationship #4 – A panacea is used to cure and a vacuum is used to clean.

2. C, relationship #8 – The "magn" and "mini" roots have opposite meanings, so we know magnificent and miniscule must be antonyms. Abstract means not clearly defined, which is the opposite of concrete.

3. B, relationship #3 – Infidelity is a type of betrayal. A clown is a type of performer.

4. E, relationship #5 – This is a degree relationship. To excise is to cut something out, but to eradicate is to get rid of it forever. To deter is to discourage someone from doing something, but to forbid is to absolutely not let him do it. You may have chosen choice A because chronicle and record are synonyms, however, one is not a more extreme form of the other, so choice A does not work.

5. B, relationship #10 – In the question words, "had" is the past tense of "have". Answer choice B works because "were" is the past tense of "are". Answer choice C might have been tempting, but the words are in the wrong order.

Reading section

Reading practice

1. E – The first sentence of the second paragraph restates choice E. Choice C is tempting because right after the passage discusses "sister planet", it mentions that Venus may have had oceans. However, it doesn't say that it was called Earth's sister planet because of those oceans, so choice C is wrong.

2. C – The passage does talk about the volcanoes on Venus. Don't be fooled by choices A and B. Oceans are not currently found on Venus, so choice A is wrong. The passage also mentions lava, but only to say that there is no lava on Venus, so choice B is also wrong.

3. A – Lines 17-19 tell us that it was Pythagoras. Choices B, C, and D are mentioned in the passage, but not as having identified the morning star and the evening star as Venus.

4. D – If we use ruling out, choice A is out because the passage tells us that there is no explanation for why Venus has volcanoes but no lava. Choice B can be eliminated because it is far broader than the scope of the passage. Choice C is out because the passage doesn't tell us where Venus' name came from. Choice E is out because comparing Venus to Earth was the topic of one paragraph, but not the entire passage. We are left with choice D, which goes well with the very last sentence of the passage.

5. B – For this one, the passage tells us that people once thought Venus was a star, but that it really isn't. That means choice B is correct.

Math section

Math practice

1. D – First we solve for T. If $T + 25 = 28$, then T must equal 3. If $T = 3$, then $T \times 25 = 3 \times 25 = 75$.

2. C – This is another one of those tricky problems that mixes units of measurement. First we have to convert 3 feet into inches, so we multiply 3×12 to get 36 inches. Now we can divide 36 by 4, which tells us how many groups of 4 inches would fit in 36 inches. $36 \div 4 = 9$, so C is our answer.

3. A – The 7 in the A place is equal to 700,000. The 7 in the B place is equal to 70. To get from 70 to 700,000, we need 4 more zeroes, so we would multiply by 10,000.

4. C – All of the angles on one side of a line add to 180°. That means that $x + x + 4x = 180$. If we combine like terms, we get $6x = 180$. In order to get x by itself, we have to divide both sides by 6. $180 \div 6 = 30$, so choice C is correct.

5. E – For this problem, we have variables in the answer choices, so we can plug in our own numbers. Since $a + b$ is divisible by 5, let's make $a = 2$ and $b = 3$. Now we plug those values into the answer choices to see which one gives a result that is divisible by 5.

(A) $a \times b = 2 \times 3 = 6$

(B) $5 + (a \times b) = 5 + (2 \times 3) = 5 + 6 = 11$

(C) $5a + 2b = 5(2) + 2(3) = 10 + 6 = 16$

(D) $\dfrac{a+b}{5} = \dfrac{2+3}{5} = 1$

(E) $(3 \times a) + (3 \times b) = (3 \times 2) + (3 \times 3) = 6 + 9 = 15$

Answer choice E gives us a value evenly divisible by 5, so it is the correct answer choice.

6. C – This question is really testing whether or not you remember to apply order of operations, or PEMDAS. We have to perform the multiplication and division operations first:

$$40 - 2(3) + 24 \div 6 = 40 - 6 + 4 = 38$$

7. C – This is a probability question, so the first thing we need to do is figure out how many possible outcomes there are. There are 60 cards, so there are 60 possible outcomes. Now we need to figure out how many of them are divisible by both 3 and 5. The trick here is that in order for a number to be divisible by both 3 and 5, it has to be a multiple of 15 (since $3 \times 5 = 15$). The multiples of 15 that are 60 or less are 15, 30, 45, and 60. Now we know that 4 out of 60 cards, or $\dfrac{4}{60}$ of the cards, are divisible by both 3 and 5. Now we divide both 4 and 60 by 4 and get that the probability of drawing a card divisible by both 3 and 5 is $\dfrac{1}{15}$.

Vocabulary

Roots

Below are some roots. I will give you the definition of each root and then two examples of words that have that root. Look up the meanings of those words and write the definitions in the blanks provided. As you look up the definition of each word, think about how it relates to the root. After you write the definition of each word, write a sentence using the word or a memory trick or association for remembering the word.

Root: *cred*
> Definition – believe

Examples:
> *Credible*
>> Definition:
>> Sentence or memory trick:
> *Creed* (Yes, I know this is spelled slightly differently than the root – it happens!)
>> Definition:
>> Sentence or memory trick:

Root: *mal*
> Definition – bad

Examples:
> *Malevolent*
>> Definition:
>> Sentence or memory trick:
> *Malady*
>> Definition:
>> Sentence or memory trick:

Word to remember!

Rancorous – characterized by hostility
Example: After Sheila's best friend stole her boyfriend, their relationship became quite rancorous.

Now, MAKE FLASHCARDS FOR ALL THE WORDS ABOVE – AND STUDY THEM!

Verbal section

Synonyms strategies

If you know the word, think of a definition before you look at answer choices.

If you have heard the word but can't define it:

1. Use context – in what sentence or phrase have you heard the word before?
2. Positive or negative – write a plus or minus sign next to the question word, rule out answer choices that are opposite or neutral.
3. Look for roots and word parts – ask yourself what other words this word looks like.

Synonyms practice

Before you circle the answer, write the strategy you used from above beside the question word.
TIME YOURSELF – THESE QUESTIONS SHOULD TAKE LESS THAN 3 MINUTES.

1. MALODOROUS: *Strategy:*
   (A) pleasantly fragrant
   (B) noisy
   (C) evil
   (D) smelly
   (E) plausible

2. INCREDIBLE: *Strategy:*
   (A) long
   (B) unbelievable
   (C) thrilled
   (D) timid
   (E) static

3. THICKEN: *Strategy:*

   (A) congeal
   (B) scull
   (C) mediate
   (D) confide
   (E) excise

4. INCISIVE: *Strategy:*

   (A) massive
   (B) simple
   (C) cutting
   (D) frugal
   (E) lively

5. DEGENERATE: *Strategy:*

   (A) clean
   (B) mark
   (C) drip
   (D) grasp
   (E) disintegrate

Analogies strategies

1. If you know the question words, make a sentence from them.

2. If you don't know the question words, go to the answer choices and:

   (A) Try to make a sentence with the answer choices. Rule out any that do not have a strong relationship. If you hear yourself using the words "can", "maybe", "could", or "sometimes", you are talking yourself into the wrong answer.

   (B) With the choices left, try to plug the question words into the sentence that you made with the answer choice words. Could it work?

3. If you are stuck on any of the last ten analogies, simply pick the answer choice with the weirdest word.

Analogies practice

Listed below are some of the common relationships used on this test:

1. Occupation – one word is the job of the other word
2. Part of – one word is a part of the other word
3. Type of – one word is a type of the other word, which is a broader category
4. Used for – one word is used to do the other word
5. Degree – the words have roughly the same meaning, only one is more extreme
6. Characteristic of – one word is a characteristic of the other
7. Synonyms – the words are synonyms
8. Antonyms – the words are opposite in meaning
9. Found in – one word is found in the other
10. Grammatical – one word has a grammatical relationship to the other

Below are sample analogy questions.

Next to each question:

(A) If you know the question words, write in the relationship number from the list above.
(B) If you don't know the question words, write in WB (for working backwards, which is what we are doing when we rule out answer choices and then guess.)

TIME YOURSELF – THESE QUESTIONS SHOULD TAKE LESS THAN 3 MINUTES.

1. Pantheon is to gods as   *Relationship # / Strategy:*
   (A) dictionary is to words
   (B) screwdriver is to screw
   (C) doctor is to nurse
   (D) winter is to summer
   (E) priest is to church

2. Health is to malady as silence is to   *Relationship # / Strategy:*

   (A) quiet
   (B) reservation
   (C) noise
   (D) furor
   (E) steam

3. Malevolent is to terrorist as   *Relationship # / Strategy:*

   (A) quiet is to scholar
   (B) crass is to performer
   (C) funny is to teacher
   (D) peaceful is to pacifist
   (E) lucky is to philanthropist

4. Rancorous is to acrimonious as   *Relationship # / Strategy:*

   (A) belligerent is to harmonious
   (B) shy is to athletic
   (C) lively is to vivacious
   (D) quiet is to determined
   (E) lax is to successful

5. Credible is to unbelievable as   *Relationship # / Strategy:*

   (A) kind is to popular
   (B) erratic is to frumpy
   (C) formidable is to weak
   (D) culpable is to blind
   (E) malevolent is to sinister

Reading section

Reading strategies

The first step when you approach each passage is to look at the questions first. You will want to label each question with either "S" or "G". If it is a specific question, label it with "S". If it is a general question, label it with "G".

Then read the passage. Answer specific questions as you go. Answer general questions at the end.

Secrets for answering specific questions:

1. You can almost always underline the correct answer in the passage for specific questions. If you can't underline your answer (often restated using synonyms), then you haven't found the right answer – keep looking!
2. The wrong answer choices often take the same words from the passage and then twist around the order so that they have a different meaning.
3. Look out for assumptions that you make that are not backed up by the passage.

Secrets for general questions:

1. They often have the words "mainly" or "primarily" in them.
2. Before answering these questions, reread the last sentence of the entire passage.
3. The wrong answers are often mentioned in the passage, but they are details and NOT the main idea.

Reading practice

Below is a practice reading passage. It is an American history passage, one of the many types that you will see on this test.

TIME YOURSELF – THIS PASSAGE AND QUESTIONS SHOULD TAKE A TOTAL OF 5 MINUTES

Samuel Adams has been both a revered and a reviled figure in American history. Those who place him on a pedestal as a true patriot point to his actions leading up to the American Revolution. According to their side of the story, Samuel Adams' speech against taxation without representation at a Boston Town
Line 5 Meeting in 1764 was designed to inspire other patriots to fight for the colonies' independence from Britain. They also view Samuel Adams as a key figure in coordinating the resistance of the colonies. To some Americans, Samuel Adams is a brave statesman leading the colonies into a war for justice.

Samuel Adams' detractors paint a vastly different picture. In 1768, Samuel
10 Adams sent a circular letter in an attempt to organize colonists against the British occupation of Boston. According to one theory, this circular letter led directly to the Boston Massacre. Samuel Adams also set up a committee of correspondence as a way to link patriots in all thirteen colonies. Some view this committee as an inflammatory group designed to encourage actions such as the Boston Tea Party,
15 and eventually war. To these historians, Samuel Adams was a propagandist in favor of violence instead of reconciliation.

The true story of Samuel Adams shows that neither side may be right. There is evidence in his papers that he wanted reform in the colonies, not a revolution. As historian Pauline Maier notes, "There is no evidence he prompted
20 the Boston Massacre Riot." What we do know is that he was a man of words, contributing to some of the most important documents in the history of the United States, such as the Declaration of Independence and the Articles of Confederation.

1. Which of the following is the best title for this selection?
   (A) Samuel Adams, a Boston Native
   (B) The American Revolution
   (C) The Boston Tea Party
   (D) Signers of the Declaration of Independence
   (E) Samuel Adams, a Misunderstood Founding Father

2. Which of the following words would the author most likely use to describe Samuel Adams?

    (A) vile
    (B) well-written
    (C) untalented
    (D) fortunate
    (E) serious

3. In line 1, when the author writes that Samuel Adams has been both "a revered and a reviled figure", it is meant that

    (A) Samuel Adams has been both respected and resented by Americans
    (B) Samuel Adams actions were deplorable
    (C) Samuel Adams was an important writer in the colonies
    (D) it is now understood that Samuel Adams was a great patriot
    (E) Samuel Adams was disliked by other Founding Fathers

4. The author suggests which of the following was Samuel Adams' true goal in sending out a circular letter?

    (A) to directly cause the Boston Tea Party
    (B) it was a rough draft of the Declaration of Independence
    (C) to encourage reform and not to instigate violence
    (D) to divide the colonies
    (E) to speak in favor of taxation without representation

5. Based on the passage, what is the author most likely to discuss next?

    (A) Samuel Adams' contributions after the Revolutionary War
    (B) other important Founding Fathers
    (C) violence in the colonies
    (D) Samuel Adams' education and background
    (E) the importance of the Boston Tea Party

Math section

Math practice

1. When 297 is divided by 32, the result is closest to which of the following?

    (A) 5
    (B) 10
    (C) 15
    (D) 20
    (E) 25

2. $0.03 \times 600.00 =$

    (A) 0.0018
    (B) 0.018
    (C) 0.18
    (D) 1.8
    (E) 18

3. The average test score for 4 students was an 80. The average for 2 other students was a 90. What was the approximate average for all 6 students?

    (A) 79
    (B) 83
    (C) 85
    (D) 87
    (E) 91

4. A telephone call costs $0.50 for the first minute and $0.10 for each additional minute. For how many minutes could a person talk if she paid $1.80?

    (A) 10
    (B) 11
    (C) 12
    (D) 13
    (E) 14

5. What is 20% of 10% of 200?

   (A) 4
   (B) 30
   (C) 60
   (D) 100
   (E) 170

6. Use the number line below to answer the question.

   What fraction does the point M represent?

   (A) $\dfrac{5}{12}$

   (B) $\dfrac{6}{12}$

   (C) $\dfrac{7}{12}$

   (D) $\dfrac{8}{12}$

   (E) $\dfrac{9}{12}$

7. 12 is what percent of 20?

   (A) 2.4%
   (B) 8%
   (C) 30%
   (D) 55%
   (E) 60%

Workout #5 Answers

Vocabulary

Look them up!

Verbal section

Synonyms practice

1. D – The root "mal" means bad, so malodorous literally means bad odor.

2. B – You have to pay close attention to roots on this one. "In" as a prefix can mean not, "cred" means believe, and "ible" means able. If you put that together, you get not able to be believed. People often say that something is "incredible" when a good thing happens, so thrilled would be a tempting choice. If we use roots, though, we know that unbelievable is a better answer.

3. A – Congeal is a word to remember from Workout #2, so make a flashcard if you missed this one.

4. C – The "cis" root means to cut, so we know that the best answer is choice C, cutting.

5. E – The "gen" root means to create, but the "de" prefix tells us that we are looking for the opposite of creating. Disintegrate means to fall apart, so it is the correct answer. If nothing else, you could guess disintegrate because it has a negative root and degenerate has a negative root as well.

Analogies practice

1. A, relationship #2 – The gods are all part of the pantheon (pantheon is the group of all the gods) and words are all part of the dictionary.

2. C, relationship #8 – A malady is an illness, so health is the opposite of malady. Silence is the opposite of noise.

3. D, relationship #6 – Malevolent means evil, so it is a characteristic of a terrorist. Peaceful is a characteristic of a pacifist, or someone who loves peace.

4. C, relationship #7 – Rancorous and acrimonious both describe bitter relationships, so they are synonyms. Lively and vivacious both describe someone who is full of life, so they are also synonyms.

5. C, relationship #8 – Credible is something that is believable, so it is the opposite of unbelievable. Formidable means strong, so it is the opposite of weak.

Reading section

Reading practice

1. E – This is a general question so we look to the last sentence. The last sentence is about his contribution to the new country. We can rule out B, C, and D because they don't even talk about Samuel Adams. The last sentence doesn't even mention Boston, so we can rule out A as well. Choice E comes closest with its reference to Samuel Adams as "Founding Father".

2. B – If we look for evidence in the passage, the only answer that we can find support for what the author thinks is the description of well-written. The author writes about other people who may have thought he was vile, but the author does not take a side in that debate.

3. A – If you don't know what reviled and revered mean, then you have to look for evidence in the passage. After using those terms as an introduction, the author discusses people who liked Samuel Adams and people who did not. Choice A captures this meaning the best.

4. C – In the last paragraph, the author includes a quote from a historian that contradicts the theory that Samuel Adams was trying to start a war. The author also tells us in the last paragraph that Samuel Adams wanted reform.

5. A – On the SSAT, questions about "what the author will discuss next" usually stick closely to what the passage is already talking about. The right answer is a continuation of thought, not a new but related subject. Only choices A and D continue the theme of Samuel Adams. It would make more sense to continue to discuss his adulthood rather than jump back to his childhood, so choice A is the best answer.

Math section

Math practice

1. B – The question said "closest to" so we can estimate. 297 is about 300 and 32 is about 30, so we can do $300 \div 30$, which gives us 10.

2. E – If we look at the answer choices, we can see that this is really a question about place value. If we multiply 3 times 600, we get 1,800. However, since we moved the decimal

two places to the right to get from 0.03 to 3, we have to move the decimal point back two places to the left. This gives us 18.

3. B – This is a weighted average question. In order to answer these questions, we can NOT just average the two averages. Rather, we have to find the sum of all the scores. If we rearrange the average equation, we get $average \times number\ of\ items = sum$. Since four students averaged an 80, the sum of their scores must be 320. Two students averaged 90, so the sum of their scores must be 180. If we add these two groups together, we get that all six of their scores add up to 500. We divide 500 by 6 and get an average of 83 and some decimal. Since this is a multiple choice test and the question says "approximately", that is as far as we need to go. We have enough information to choose B.

4. E – The first minute costs \$0.50, so the remaining minutes would cost \$1.30. At \$0.10 a minute, you would get 13 minutes for \$1.30. When we add in that first minute, we get a total of 14 minutes.

5. A – We actually have to start at the end and work backward with this type of question. 10% of 200 is 20. Then we take 20% of that. 10% of 20 is 2, so 20% of 20 is 4.

6. C – If we look at our answer choices, we can see that all of them are fractions with a denominator of 12. This tells us that we should convert the fractions that come before and after point M into equivalent fractions that have 12 as their denominators. If we convert $\frac{1}{2}$ into $\frac{6}{12}$ and $\frac{2}{3}$ into $\frac{8}{12}$, we can see that point M has a value of $\frac{7}{12}$.

7. E – Our first step is to translate the words into equation language. The word "is" represents an equal sign, "what percent" can be translated into $\frac{x}{100}$, and the word "of" represents multiplication:

$$12 = \frac{x}{100} \times 20$$

If we solve for x, we get that $x = 60$ or 60%.

Vocabulary

Roots

This is a vocabulary review. Be sure to study the meanings of the roots we have covered before you attempt this section.

Roots review – Next to each root below, write the meaning.

1. *de* _____
2. *cis* _____
3. *fid* _____
4. *pan* _____
5. *loc / loq / log* _____
6. *magna* _____
7. *bene* _____
8. *chron* _____
9. *cred* _____
10. *mal* _____

Verbal section

Synonyms strategies

If you know the word, think of a definition before you look at answer choices.

If you have heard the word but can't define it:

1. Use context – in what sentence or phrase have you heard the word before?
2. Positive or negative – write a plus or minus sign next to the question word, rule out answer choices that are opposite or neutral.
3. Look for roots and word parts – ask yourself what other words this word looks like.

Synonyms practice

Before you circle the answer, write the strategy you used beside the question word.
TIME YOURSELF – THESE QUESTIONS SHOULD TAKE LESS THAN 3 MINUTES.

1. FRUGAL: *Strategy:*

   (A) pleasant
   (B) distant
   (C) restless
   (D) economical
   (E) functional

2. CONGEAL: *Strategy:*

   (A) lose
   (B) harden
   (C) entrust
   (D) torture
   (E) carry

3. TACT: *Strategy:*

   (A) sensitivity
   (B) rudeness
   (C) confusion
   (D) turn
   (E) rerun

4. SCULL: *Strategy:*

   (A) brain
   (B) toast
   (C) boat
   (D) life
   (E) autumn

5. RANCOROUS: *Strategy:*

    (A) harmonious

    (B) loud

    (C) fun

    (D) somber

    (E) bitter

Analogies strategies

1. If you know the question words, make a sentence from them.

2. If you don't know the question words, go to the answer choices and:

    (A) Try to make a sentence with the answer choices. Rule out any that do not have a strong relationship. If you hear yourself using the words "can", "maybe", "could", or "sometimes", you are talking yourself into the wrong answer.

    (B) With the choices left, try to plug the question words into the sentence that you made with the answer choice words. Could it work?

3. If you are stuck on any of the last ten analogies, simply pick the answer choice with the weirdest word.

Analogies practice

Listed below are some of the common relationships used on this test:

1. Occupation – one word is the job of the other word

2. Part of – one word is a part of the other word

3. Type of – one word is a type of the other word, which is a broader category

4. Used for – one word is used to do the other word

5. Degree – the words have roughly the same meaning, only one is more extreme

6. Characteristic of – one word is a characteristic of the other

7. Synonyms – the words are synonyms

8. Antonyms – the words are opposite in meaning

9. Found in – one word is found in the other

10. Grammatical – one word has a grammatical relationship to the other

Below are sample analogy questions.

Next to each question:

(A) If you know the question words, write in the relationship number from the preceding list.
(B) If you don't know the question words, write in WB (for working backwards, which is what we are doing when we rule out answer choices and then guess.)

TIME YOURSELF – THESE QUESTIONS SHOULD TAKE LESS THAN 3 MINUTES.

1. Beneficent is to evil as   *Relationship # / Strategy:*

    (A) belt is to dress
    (B) ascent is to descent
    (C) swimmer is to water
    (D) church is to temple
    (E) circle is to square

2. Deter is to encourage as irritate is to   *Relationship # / Strategy:*

    (A) soothe
    (B) build
    (C) annoy
    (D) renounce
    (E) stunning

3. Deflate is to collapse as   *Relationship # / Strategy:*

    (A) exhibit is to paint
    (B) rattle is to noise
    (C) inflate is to explode
    (D) judge is to explain
    (E) run is to jog

4. Beneficial is to favorable as   *Relationship # / Strategy:*

    (A) irate is to calm
    (B) jovial is to energetic
    (C) conceited is to attractive
    (D) detrimental is to harmful
    (E) volatile is to rough

5. Incredulous is to skeptic as   *Relationship # / Strategy:*

   (A) praise is to critic
   (B) fast is to runner
   (C) tedious is to police
   (D) admiring is to teacher
   (E) frugal is to miser

Reading section

Reading strategies

The first step when you approach each passage is to look at the questions first. You will want to label each question with either "S" or "G". If it is a specific question, label it with "S". If it is a general question, label it with "G".

Then read the passage. Answer specific questions as you go. Answer general questions at the end.

Secrets for answering specific questions:

1. You can almost always underline the correct answer in the passage for specific questions. If you can't underline your answer (often restated using synonyms), then you haven't found the right answer – keep looking!
2. The wrong answer choices often take the same words from the passage and then twist around the order so that they have a different meaning.
3. Look out for assumptions that you make that are not backed up by the passage.

Secrets for general questions:

1. They often have the words "mainly" or "primarily" in them.
2. Before answering these questions, reread the last sentence of the entire passage.
3. The wrong answers are often mentioned in the passage, but they are details and NOT the main idea.

Reading practice

Below is a practice reading passage. It is an American history document, one of the many types of passages that you will see on this test.

TIME YOURSELF – THIS PASSAGE AND QUESTIONS SHOULD TAKE A TOTAL OF 5 MINUTES

The following part of a speech was given by Frederick Douglass in 1852 on the Fourth of July.

Line 5
Fellow citizens, above your national, tumultuous joy, I hear the mournful wail of millions, whose chains, heavy and grievous yesterday, are today rendered more intolerable by the jubilant shouts that reach them. If I do forget, if I do not remember those bleeding children of sorrow this day, "may my right hand forget her cunning, and may my tongue cleave to the roof of my mouth!"

10
To forget them, to pass lightly over their wrongs and to chime in with the popular theme would be treason most scandalous and shocking, and would make me a reproach before God and the world.

My subject, then, fellow citizens, is "American Slavery." I shall see this day and its popular characteristics from the slave's point of view. Standing here, identified with the American bondman, making his wrongs mine, I do not hesitate

15
to declare, with all my soul, that the character and conduct of this nation never looked blacker to me than on this Fourth of July.

1. Why does Frederick Douglass say that the "conduct of this nation never looked blacker to me than on this Fourth of July" in lines 15-16?

   (A) He was speaking to an audience of slave hunters.
   (B) Most of the people to whom he was speaking were not able to help slaves.
   (C) Slavery still existed in the United States at the time of his speech.
   (D) The Declaration of Independence had promised slaves freedom but they had not yet received it.
   (E) He is personally a slave owner.

2. What does Frederick Douglass mean when he says that the chains "are today rendered more intolerable by the jubilant shouts that reach them" in lines 5-6?

   (A) Those who are slaves feel more oppressed when they hear other Americans celebrating their freedom.
   (B) The slave masters make the slaves work longer hours since it is a holiday.
   (C) It shows that slaves are not enjoying the freedom that they have been given.
   (D) The audience members should not be bothered by the sound of the chains.
   (E) The slaves are loudly celebrating in their own quarters.

3. The purpose of Frederick Douglass' speech was to

   (A) rally the slaves to revolt
   (B) ruin the fun that the audience was having
   (C) suggest that people should go home and free their slaves immediately
   (D) point out the injustice of other Americans celebrating their freedom while slaves remain captive
   (E) encourage the party to end early

4. What is the "popular theme" to which Frederick Douglas was referring in line 10?

   (A) abolishing slavery
   (B) giving women the right to vote
   (C) freedom and independence
   (D) fireworks
   (E) western expansion

Math section

Math practice

TIME YOURSELF – THESE PROBLEMS SHOULD TAKE YOU ABOUT 9 MINUTES TOTAL.

1. $40 - 3\frac{4}{15} =$

   (A) $36\frac{4}{15}$

   (B) $36\frac{11}{15}$

   (C) $37\frac{4}{15}$

   (D) $37\frac{2}{3}$

   (E) $38\frac{2}{3}$

2. The average test score for two students was 80. The average test score for another three students was an 85. What was the average for all five students?

   (A) 79
   (B) 81
   (C) 82.5
   (D) 83
   (E) 84

3. 6 is 8 percent of

   (A) 36
   (B) 48
   (C) 75
   (D) 92
   (E) 100

4. $0.1725 =$

   (A) $\dfrac{1}{10} + \dfrac{7}{100} + \dfrac{2}{1,000} + \dfrac{5}{10,000}$

   (B) $\dfrac{1}{10} \times \dfrac{7}{100} \times \dfrac{2}{1,000} \times \dfrac{5}{10,000}$

   (C) $\dfrac{17}{10} + \dfrac{25}{100}$

   (D) $1 + \dfrac{1}{7} + \dfrac{1}{1} + \dfrac{1}{5}$

   (E) $\dfrac{1}{10} + \dfrac{7}{10} + \dfrac{2}{10} + \dfrac{5}{10}$

5. If $a > 5$, which of the following is greatest?

   (A) $\dfrac{a+5}{a}$

   (B) $\dfrac{a}{a+5}$

   (C) $a + 5$

   (D) $a - 5$

   (E) $3a + 5$

6. The sum of two numbers, whose difference is 6, is 35. Which equation could be used to find the larger number?

   (A) $2x + 6 = 35$

   (B) $x + 2x + 6 = 35$

   (C) $x + x - 6 = 35$

   (D) $x - (x + 6) = 35$

   (E) $x - (x - 6) = 35$

7. In the figure below, point O is the center of a circle, points L and M are on the circle and are the vertices of a triangle, and the measure of angle LOM is 90 degrees.

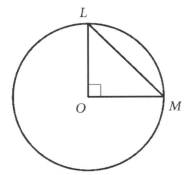

If the area of the circle is 36π cm^2, then what is the area of triangle LOM?

(A) 9 cm^2

(B) 18 cm^2

(C) 24 cm^2

(D) 28 cm^2

(E) 36 cm^2

Workout #6 Answers

Vocabulary

Roots

1. opposite of or away from
2. to cut
3. trust or faith
4. all
5. to speak
6. big
7. good or well
8. time
9. believe
10. bad

Verbal section

Synonyms practice

1. D – Frugal is a word to remember from Workout #1. Please review these words if you missed this question.

2. B – Congeal is a word to remember from Workout #2. Please review these words if you missed this question.

3. A – Tact means not wanting to offend, and choice A comes closest to this meaning. Tact is a word to remember from Workout #3.

4. C – Don't be tricked by this one. Scull spelled with a "c" is a type of boat used to race crew. This is a word to remember from Workout #4.

5. E – Rancor is bad feelings, so rancorous describes a relationship characterized by bitter feelings. This is a word to remember from Workout #5.

Analogies practice

1. B, relationship #8 – Beneficent and evil are opposites (the "bene" root means good, which is the opposite of evil). Ascent and descent are also opposites, as we can tell from the prefixes.

2. A, relationship #8 – Deter has a negative root and encourage is a positive word, so even without knowing the exact meaning of deter we can make a good guess that encourage and deter are opposite in meaning. Soothe is the opposite of irritate, so choice A is correct.

3. C, relationship #5 – To deflate is to slowly let the air out of something, but if something is really deflated, it collapses. If something is really inflated, it explodes, so choice C is correct.

4. D, relationship #7 – The "bene" root means good, so beneficial and favorable are synonyms. Detrimental and harmful are also synonyms. With this question, we have to be careful to look for true synonyms and not just words that "seem to go together". Jovial and energetic could be related and conceited people may be attractive, but these words are not synonyms, so choices B and C are not correct.

5. E, relationship #6 – We can use roots to determine the first relationship. "In" can mean not as a prefix and "cred" means to believe. If someone does not believe, they are incredulous. This is a characteristic of a skeptic. A characteristic of a miser is frugality, so choice E is correct. A teacher may be admiring, but not always. A runner may be fast, but he may also be slow. Only a miser is always frugal.

Reading section

Reading practice

1. C – Remember that we have to have evidence. We have no idea to whom he was speaking, so we can rule out choices A and B. The passage also does not mention the Declaration of Independence or whether or not Douglass owned slaves, so choices D and E are out. He does talk about not forgetting the slaves who are chained, however, so we can assume that slavery existed at the time.

2. A – Again, if the answer is very specific, then we have to have evidence. If you look at choice B, there is not evidence that the slaves are working longer hours (although we may make that assumption, the passage does not give us support for it). Choice B can be eliminated. Choice C can be ruled out because Douglass is saying that the slaves have not been given freedom. If you look at choice D, Douglass is saying the opposite. He is

telling the audience that the chains should bother them. Choice E can also be eliminated because the slaves are producing a "mournful wail" and not celebrating. This leaves us with choice A, which goes along with the theme of the passage.

3. D – Choices A and C are too extreme. Choices B and E imply that one of the greatest Americans of all time was merely there to spoil the fun, which would definitely not be the right answer on the SSAT. We are left with choice D.

4. C – Douglass gave this speech on the Fourth of July, so the theme of the day would have been independence. Choice D (fireworks) is a trap. We may associate the Fourth of July and fireworks, but that is not the focus of Douglass' speech.

Math section

Math practice

1. B – We can use our range strategy on this one. $3\frac{4}{15}$ is between 3 and 4. $40 - 3 = 37$ and $40 - 4 = 36$. This tells us that the correct answer is between 36 and 37, so we know that it must be A or B. A is a trap – when you subtract a fraction, you generally do not wind up with the same fraction. If you find a common denominator and do the math, choice B is correct.

2. D – This is a weighted average problem. Our first step is to find the sum of all the scores. The first group has two students with an average of 80, so the sum of their scores is 160. The second group has three students with an average of 85, so the sum of their scores is 255. If we add these numbers together, we get that the sum of all five students' scores is 415. To find the average, we divide 415 by 5. This gives us an average of 83.

3. C – You can estimate and plug in answer choices to see what works. 8% is about 10%, so you can find 10% of each answer choice.

    (A) 10% of 36 is 3.6
    (B) 10% of 48 is 4.8
    (C) 10% of 75 is 7.5
    (D) 10% of 92 is 9.2
    (E) 10% of 100 is 10

    Since 8% is a little less than 10%, I am looking for something that is a little bit bigger than 6. Choice C fits the bill.

4. A – This question tests place value. The first place to the right of the decimal point is the tenths place, the next one is the hundredths place, the next one is the thousandths place,

and the one after that is the ten-thousandths place. Choice A correctly assigns the value of each digit in the number.

5. E – For this question, there are variables in the answer choices, so we can plug in our own number. The problem says that a is greater than 5, so we can plug 6 into the answer choices.

(A) $\dfrac{a+5}{a} = \dfrac{6+5}{6} = \dfrac{11}{6}$

(B) $\dfrac{a}{a+5} = \dfrac{6}{6+5} = \dfrac{6}{11}$

(C) $a + 5 = 6 + 5 = 11$

(D) $a - 5 = 6 - 5 = 1$

(E) $3a + 5 = 3(6) + 5 = 23$

6. C – Our first step is to make sure that we are setting x equal to the right number. The question asks for the larger number, so we set x equal to the larger number. The smaller number is therefore $x - 6$. Answer choice C correctly shows x and $x - 6$ being added together for a sum of 35.

7. B – This question requires working backward from what we are given. We start with the area of the circle, which is 36π cm^2. Since the area of a circle is equal to πr^2, where r is the radius, we can see that the radius must be 6 in order for r^2 to be equal to 36. If the radius of the circle is 6, then the length of OM and LO must be 6. Since these are the base and the height of the triangle, we can plug them into the formula:

$$area\ of\ triangle = \frac{1}{2}(b \times h)$$

Since $\frac{1}{2}(6 \times 6) = 18$, answer choice B is correct.

Workout #7

Vocabulary

Roots

Below are some roots. I will give you the definition of each root and then two examples of words that have that root. Look up the meanings of those words and write the definitions in the blanks provided. As you look up the definition of each word, think about how it relates to the root. After you write the definition of each word, write a sentence using the word or a memory trick or association for remembering the word.

Root: *eu*

    Definition – well or good

Examples:

    Eulogy (Do you recognize the "log" root?)

        Definition:

        Sentence or memory trick:

    Euphony

        Definition:

        Sentence or memory trick:

Root: *neo / nov*

    Definition – new (Do you remember this root from neologism?)

Examples:

    Neophyte

        Definition:

        Sentence or memory trick:

    Novice

        Definition:

        Sentence or memory trick:

Word to remember!

Obsolete – out of date and therefore not useful

Example: The teenager whined to her parents that her cell phone was horribly obsolete and she needed a new one.

Now, MAKE FLASHCARDS FOR ALL THE WORDS ABOVE – AND STUDY THEM!

Verbal section

Synonyms practice

TIME YOURSELF – THESE QUESTIONS SHOULD TAKE LESS THAN 3 MINUTES.

1. INNOVATE:

   (A) flood
   (B) evict
   (C) sign
   (D) invent
   (E) praise

2. EUPHONY:

   (A) loud noise
   (B) pleasant sound
   (C) drill
   (D) call
   (E) uproar

3. BITTER:

   (A) rancorous
   (B) methodical
   (C) obsolete
   (D) profound
   (E) residual

4. EUPHORIA:

   (A) tact
   (B) load
   (C) jubilation
   (D) sound
   (E) felon

5. MALFUNCTIONING:

   (A) operating
   (B) ignoring
   (C) flight
   (D) mean
   (E) defective

Synonyms strategies checklist

Check off the strategies that you used. If you didn't use any of these strategies, go back and look over your work!

Did you…   Yes   No

1. Use roots to figure out meaning?   ____   ____
2. Use context?   ____   ____
3. Use positive or negative?   ____   ____
4. Rule out what you could and then guess?   ____   ____

Analogies practice

TIME YOURSELF – THESE QUESTIONS SHOULD TAKE LESS THAN 3 MINUTES.

1. Obsolete is to novel as

   (A) friendly is to grumpy
   (B) humorous is to funny
   (C) unique is to solitary
   (D) liberated is to free
   (E) ideal is to uneasy

2. Tyrannical is to benevolent as impatient is to

   (A) crowded
   (B) understanding
   (C) boring
   (D) beneficial
   (E) expert

3. Eloquent is to orator as

   (A) praiseworthy is to criminal
   (B) frantic is to teacher
   (C) devoted is to indigent
   (D) conceited is to actress
   (E) beneficent to philanthropist

4. Epidemic is to pandemic as

   (A) mansion is to house
   (B) house is to home
   (C) protest is to riot
   (D) funnel is to cake
   (E) rain is to precipitation

5. Novice is to beginner as

   (A) sail is to boat
   (B) expert is to force
   (C) foundation is to roof
   (D) bend is to curve
   (E) saint is to villain

Analogies strategies checklist

Check off the strategies that you used. If you didn't use any of these strategies, go back and look over your work!

Did you...   Yes   No

1. Identify the relationship if you knew the words?   ____   ____

2. Go to the answer choices and rule out the ones
    that were not related or that couldn't have
    the same relationship as the question words
    if you didn't know the words?   ____   ____

3. Guess if you could rule out even one?   ____   ____

Reading section

Reading practice

Below is a practice reading passage. It is a poetry passage, one of the many types that you will see on this test.

TIME YOURSELF – THIS PASSAGE AND QUESTIONS SHOULD TAKE A TOTAL OF 5 MINUTES

Have you got a brook in your little heart,
Where bashful flowers blow,
And blushing birds go down to drink,
And shadows tremble so?

Line 5

And nobody knows, so still it flows,
That any brook is there;
And yet your little draught of life
Is daily drunken there.

10

Then look out for the little brook in March,
When the rivers overflow,
And the snows come hurrying from the hills,
And the bridges often go.

15

And later, in August it may be,
When the meadows parching lie,
Beware, lest this little brook of life
Some burning noon go dry!

20

– Emily Dickinson

1. In this poem, the little brook most probably represents

   (A) a deep, dark secret
   (B) a passion that is kept secret
   (C) a strong river
   (D) the autumn migration of birds
   (E) death

2. Which of the following statements would the speaker of the poem most likely agree with?

   (A) People should keep not let the love in their hearts die out.
   (B) People should keep love a secret.
   (C) People should keep wells so that they will not run out of water in a drought.
   (D) Love is better when it is out in the open.
   (E) Visiting nature is like falling in love.

3. "Where bashful flowers blow" (line 2) suggests

   (A) receiving flowers is generally embarrassing
   (B) flowers are hard to grow next to a river
   (C) people have a part of their hearts that they are too nervous to share with others
   (D) the brook will swamp the flowers in the spring
   (E) a late snow can sometimes kill the flowers

4. Why do the "rivers overflow" (line 12)?

   (A) It rained a lot.
   (B) The snow is melting in the mountains.
   (C) The speaker is angry.
   (D) Other rivers are overflowing.
   (E) The rivers did not overflow.

Reading strategies checklist

Check off the strategies that you used. If you didn't use any of these strategies, go back and look over your work!

Did you…   Yes   No

1. Mark "S" and "G"?   ____ ____

2. Reread the last sentences before answering
   general questions (although this is
   less helpful on a poetry passage)?   ____ ____

3. Underline the answers in the passage
   for specific questions?   ____ ____

Math section

Math practice

TIME YOURSELF – THESE PROBLEMS SHOULD TAKE YOU ABOUT 9 MINUTES TOTAL.

1. If Sam has 24 baseball cards and Hannah has 32 baseball cards, how many baseball cards must Hannah give to Sam in order for them to have the same number of cards?

    (A) 8
    (B) 6
    (C) 5
    (D) 4
    (E) 2

2. Craig has a deck of cards that are numbered one through thirteen. If he randomly picks a card, what is the chance that the card will have an odd number on it?

    (A) $\dfrac{6}{13}$

    (B) $\dfrac{1}{2}$

    (C) $\dfrac{7}{13}$

    (D) $\dfrac{8}{13}$

    (E) $\dfrac{2}{3}$

3. At a restaurant, 24 people are waiting to be seated. There are eight tables available. If each table has at least one person but no table has more than five people, what is the maximum number of tables that can have five people?

    (A) 6
    (B) 5
    (C) 4
    (D) 3
    (E) 2

$$25{,}193 \times 1{,}107$$

4. The result of the above expression is closest to:
   - (A) 37,500,000
   - (B) 25,000,000
   - (C) 3,750,000
   - (D) 2,500,000
   - (E) 375,000

5. If the average of 7 consecutive odd whole numbers is 13, what is the largest of these numbers?
   - (A) 7
   - (B) 10
   - (C) 13
   - (D) 16
   - (E) 19

6. The coordinate points $(2, -3)$ and $(5, m)$ are on a line that is perpendicular to the line $y = x + 2$. What is the value of m?
   - (A) -6
   - (B) -3
   - (C) -1
   - (D) 3
   - (E) 6

7. $\frac{2}{3}$ of $\frac{3}{5}$ is equal to
   - (A) $\frac{2}{15}$
   - (B) $\frac{2}{5}$
   - (C) $\frac{1}{2}$
   - (D) $\frac{5}{8}$
   - (E) $\frac{19}{15}$

Workout #7 Answers

Vocabulary

Look them up!

Verbal section

Synonyms practice

1. D – The "nov" root means new, so innovate means to make something new, or invent.

2. B – "Eu" means well or good and "phon" means sound (think of telephone), so euphony is a pleasant sound.

3. A – Rancorous is a synonym for bitter. Even if you didn't remember this, you should have been able to rule out some of the other answer choices and then guessed. Rancorous is a word to remember from Workout #5.

4. C – "Eu" means well or good, so we are looking for a positive word. Jubilation means extreme happiness, so that goes with euphoria.

5. E – "Mal" means bad, so malfunctioning means bad functioning, or defective.

Analogies practice

1. A – Obsolete means out of date, but novel (see the "nov" root) means new, so the words are antonyms. Friendly and grumpy are the only other antonyms in this question.

2. B – Tyrannical means really mean (think of Tyrannosaurus rex), but benevolent has the "bene" root which means good. This tells us that we are looking for antonyms. Understanding is the opposite of impatient, so that is our correct answer. It is not an exact match, but it is the best answer offered.

3. E – Eloquent is a characteristic of an orator (someone who gives speeches). Did you recognize the "loq" root? Choices A and C have words that are not related, so we can rule those out. A teacher may be frantic and an actress may be conceited, but the word "may" tells us that choices B and D are out as well. We are left with choice E. A philanthropist is someone who gives money to charities, so it goes with the "bene" root.

4. C – This is a degree relationship. An epidemic can grow into a pandemic (a disease that infects the whole Earth). You may have chosen choice A because a mansion is a really

big house, but the problem is that the words are in the wrong order, so choice A is out. A protest can grow into a riot, just like an epidemic can grow into a pandemic, so choice C is correct.

5. D – Novice and beginner are synonyms (did you recognize the "nov" root that means new?). A bend and a curve are also synonyms, so choice D is correct.

Reading section

Reading practice

1. B – The poem says the brook is "in your little heart" and that "nobody knows", so it is some sort of secret. We can narrow it down to choice A or B. Choice A is pretty extreme, though, with the words "deep, dark". There is nothing to indicate that it is a dark secret, so choice A is out and choice B is correct.

2. A – This is a poem, so the answer is likely metaphorical and not a literal stream running dry. The poem refers to "a brook in your little heart" and then warns us "beware, lest this little brook of life… go dry". Choice A is in line with these ideas.

3. C – Again, we need to look for the metaphorical and not the literal. Choice C is the only answer that does not talk about the literal, physical flowers, so it is the correct answer.

4. B – The poet tells us "when the rivers overflow, / And the snows come hurrying from the hills, / And the bridges often go." The snow is melting in the mountains and flooding the bridges, so choice B is correct.

Math section

Math practice

1. D – This question is asking us for the value of a variable. Even though the problem does not assign the variable a letter, the number of cards is still a variable. That means we can plug in answer choices. We will start with C because it is the middle value. If Hannah gave Sam 5 baseball cards, then she would have 27 cards and Sam would have 29 cards. This tells us that she needs to give him fewer cards. Let's try choice D. If Hannah gave Sam 4 cards, then she would have 28 cards and Sam would have 28 cards. Choice D works.

2. C – If you list out the numbers 1 through 13, you will see that there are 7 odd numbers (1, 3, 5, 7, 9, 11, and 13). That tells us that the probability of choosing an odd number is 7 out of 13, or $\frac{7}{13}$.

3. C – Go ahead and draw out the tables. Draw 8 circles. In order to get the maximum number of tables of 5, we need to have the other tables seat the minimum number of people, or just one person. If we put 5 people at one table, and one person at the other 7 tables, then we get just 12 people. Not enough. So try 2 tables of 5 and 6 tables of 1. This gives us 16 people, still not enough. If you keep doing this, you will find that when you get 4 tables of 5 and 4 tables of 1, then it adds up to 24 people, so the maximum number of tables with 5 people is 4.

4. B – We can round off for this problem since we have the words "closest to". We can multiply 25,000 × 1,000, which is equal to 25,000,0000, or choice B.

5. E – Since these are consecutive odd numbers, we know that 13 is the middle number. That means that there should be 3 numbers that are larger than 13. If we count up, we get 15, then 17, then 19. Since the problem asks for the largest number, 19, or choice E, is the correct answer.

6. A – The most important word in this question is "perpendicular". Whenever we see the word "perpendicular", we almost always need to use the fact that the slopes of perpendicular lines are negative reciprocals of one another. Since the slope of $y = x + 2$ is 1 (when there is no written coefficient of x, the implied coefficient is 1), we know that the slope of the perpendicular line must be -1. Now we can plug the points we have into the formula for slope.

$$slope = \frac{y_1 - y_2}{x_1 - x_2} = \frac{-3 - m}{2 - 5} = -1$$

    Now we can plug in our answer choices to see which one gives us -1 for $\frac{-3-m}{2-5}$ or $\frac{-3-m}{-3}$. When we plug in choice A (-6) for m, we get -1.

7. B – The key to answering this question is to recognize that the word "of" indicates that we should perform multiplication. Therefore, "$\frac{2}{3}$ of $\frac{3}{5}$" can be translated as $\frac{2}{3} \times \frac{3}{5}$. If we perform this operation, we get $\frac{2}{3} \times \frac{3}{5} = \frac{6}{15}$. This isn't one of our answer choices, so we know we must now reduce. We can divide both 6 and 15 by 3 to get $\frac{6}{15} = \frac{2}{5}$, or answer choice B.

Workout #8

Vocabulary

Roots

Below are some roots. I will give you the definition of each root and then two examples of words that have that root. Look up the meanings of those words and write the definitions in the blanks provided. As you look up the definition of each word, think about how it relates to the root. After you write the definition of each word, write a sentence using the word or a memory trick or association for remembering the word.

Root: *bio*
Definition – life
Examples:
Antibiotics
Definition:
Sentence or memory trick:
Biography
Definition:
Sentence or memory trick:

Root: *fract*
Definition – to break
Examples:
Fracture
Definition:
Sentence or memory trick:
Infraction
Definition:
Sentence or memory trick:

Word to remember!

Exacerbate – to make a problem worse

Example: I was already running late when a flat tire exacerbated my tardiness.

Now, MAKE FLASHCARDS FOR ALL THE WORDS ABOVE – AND STUDY THEM!

Verbal section

Synonyms practice

TIME YOURSELF – THESE QUESTIONS SHOULD TAKE LESS THAN 3 MINUTES.

1. CREDO:

    (A) philosophy

    (B) evasion

    (C) enjoyment

    (D) convert

    (E) predict

2. DISMAL:

    (A) friendly

    (B) angry

    (C) essential

    (D) confused

    (E) gloomy

3. INFRACTION:

    (A) necessity

    (B) transformation

    (C) violation

    (D) inscription

    (E) approval

4. PANDEMONIUM:

   (A) attack

   (B) fatigue

   (C) chaos

   (D) party

   (E) attempt

5. EXACERBATE:

   (A) lose

   (B) worsen

   (C) dispense

   (D) reform

   (E) translate

Synonyms strategies checklist

Check off the strategies that you used. If you didn't use any of these strategies, go back and look over your work!

Did you…   Yes   No

   1. Use roots to figure out meaning?   ____   ____

   2. Use context?   ____   ____

   3. Use positive or negative?   ____   ____

   4. Rule out what you could and then guess?   ____   ____

Analogies practice

TIME YOURSELF – THESE QUESTIONS SHOULD TAKE LESS THAN 3 MINUTES.

   1. Monologue is to speech as

   (A) knee is to leg

   (B) play is to scene

   (C) animal is to tiger

   (D) scull is to boat

   (E) rancor is to hostility

2. Malcontent is to unsatisfied as jubilant is to

   (A) frustrated
   (B) happy
   (C) solemn
   (D) knowledgeable
   (E) credible

3. Spill is to spilled as

   (A) run is to ran
   (B) jog is to jogging
   (C) called is to call
   (D) missed is to missing
   (E) crave is to want

4. Neonate is to toddler as

   (A) baby is to crib
   (B) rebellion is to revolution
   (C) adolescent is to adult
   (D) city is to town
   (E) pipe is to plumber

5. Biologist is to life as

   (A) forecaster is to astronomy
   (B) physicist is to malady
   (C) principal is to students
   (D) benefactor is to library
   (E) ecologist is to nature

Analogies strategies checklist

Check off the strategies that you used. If you didn't use any of these strategies, go back and look over your work!

Did you...   Yes   No

1. Identify the relationship if you knew the words?   ____   ____

2. Go to the answer choices and rule out the ones
   that were not related or that couldn't have
   the same relationship as the question words
   if you didn't know the words?   ____   ____

3. Guess if you could rule out even one?   ____   ____

Reading section

Reading practice

Below is a practice reading passage. It is a passage about native rituals, one of the many types of passages you will see on the test.

TIME YOURSELF – THIS PASSAGE AND QUESTIONS SHOULD TAKE A TOTAL OF 5 MINUTES

> The sweat lodge has a long tradition in many cultures. In Mexico, it is called the Temazcal. This is the name that the ancient Aztecs gave to the sweat lodges that they used for medicinal purposes. Sweat lodges are also present in many other cultures, such as the Scandinavian sauna or the baths of ancient Rome.
>
> Line 5 The Temazcal, however, are not used for ceremonial purposes or relaxation, but rather for curing medical complaints.
>
> There is also a spiritual element of the Temazcal. The sweat lodges are oriented to coincide with the cosmic directions described in Aztec mythology. The fire is built on the eastern side of the lodge since that is where the Aztecs believe
>
> 10 that our father, the Sun, rises. The door faces to the south. The south is considered the "pathway of the dead", which begins with birth and ends with death. The center of the sweat lodge is considered to be the mother's womb.

1. This passage is primarily about

    (A)   the history of the Aztec people
    (B)   sweat lodges in various cultures
    (C)   the Temazcal tradition
    (D)   the oppression of the Aztec people by the Spanish invaders
    (E)   the Scandinavian sauna

2. According to the passage, all are important to the Temazcal tradition EXCEPT

    (A)   the location of the door
    (B)   relaxation
    (C)   the location of the fire within the sweat lodge
    (D)   curing medical ailments
    (E)   the center of the lodge representing the mother's womb

3. The attitude of the writer toward the subject is

    (A)   harsh
    (B)   hesitant
    (C)   carefree
    (D)   interested
    (E)   ambivalent

4. It is suggested by the passage that sweat lodges in other cultures are

    (A)   used for relaxation and ceremonial purposes
    (B)   used only for medicinal purposes
    (C)   dangerous
    (D)   oriented according to the cardinal directions
    (E)   not a part of traditional culture

5. According to the passage, the doorway of the Temazcal

          I.   faces the "pathway of the dead"
          II.   represents only death
          III. leads to a place representing the womb

    (A)   I only
    (B)   I and II only
    (C)   III only
    (D)   I and III only
    (E)   I, II, and III

Reading strategies checklist

Check off the strategies that you used. If you didn't use any of these strategies, go back and look over your work!

Did you...   Yes   No

1. Mark "S" and "G"?   ____   ____

2. Reread the last sentences before answering
   general questions?   ____   ____

3. Underline the answers in the passage
   for specific questions?   ____   ____

Math section

Math practice

TIME YOURSELF – THESE PROBLEMS SHOULD TAKE YOU ABOUT 9 MINUTES TOTAL

1. Which of the following is less than $\frac{3}{4}$?

   (A) $\frac{6}{8}$

   (B) $\frac{10}{12}$

   (C) $\frac{18}{23}$

   (D) $\frac{26}{36}$

   (E) $\frac{33}{44}$

2. A weather forecaster claimed to have an 80% accuracy rate in his prediction of snowstorms. Last winter, he predicted there would be 20 snowstorms. If his accuracy rate claim is correct, and there were no snowstorms that he did not predict, how many snowstorms were there actually?

    (A) 10
    (B) 12
    (C) 16
    (D) 18
    (E) 20

3. A builder needs 62 wooden boards. If the boards only come in bundles of 12, how many bundles must he buy in order to ensure he has enough wood?

    (A) 5
    (B) 6
    (C) 8
    (D) 10
    (E) 12

4. A football team wants to add lights to their field. The dimensions of the outer perimeter of their field are 140 yards by 80 yards. If they want to place a light every 20 yards around this perimeter, how many lights will they need?

    (A) 22
    (B) 60
    (C) 80
    (D) 100
    (E) 110

5. If $3g + 6 > 15$, which of the following could NOT be g?

    (A) 3
    (B) 3.5
    (C) 4
    (D) 4.5
    (E) 6

6. Evaluate: $40 - (6^2) \div 9 + 8$

   (A) $8\frac{4}{9}$

   (B) 12

   (C) 26

   (D) 36

   (E) 44

7. On day 1 of recycling month, Troy collected 2 plastic bottles. On day 2 he collected 5 plastic bottles, on day 3 he collected 8 bottles, and on day 4 he collected 11 bottles. If this pattern continues, how many bottles will Troy collect on day 17 of recycling month?

   (A) 3

   (B) 17

   (C) 49

   (D) 50

   (E) 53

Workout #8 Answers

Vocabulary

Look them up!

Verbal section

Synonyms practice

1. A – Credo has the root "cred" in it, which means to believe. A philosophy is something that you believe in.

2. E – "Dis" and "mal" are both negative roots. We can rule out choice A because it is positive and choice C because it is neutral. If you had to guess from there, you should still guess. Dismal does mean gloomy. Think about dismal weather as context.

3. C – "Frac" means to break and an infraction occurs when the rules are broken. It is a violation.

4. C – "Pan" means all, and pandemonium occurs when everything goes crazy, so chaos is the correct answer.

5. B – If you exacerbate a problem, you make it worse, so choice B is correct.

Analogies practice

1. D – A monologue is a type of speech given by one person. A scull is a type of boat rowed by one person.

2. B – Malcontent and unsatisfied are synonyms, and jubilant is a synonym for happy.

3. A – This is a grammatical relationship. Spilled is the past tense of spill and ran is the past tense of run.

4. C – This is a sequence relationship. This is not one of our common relationships, but it does occasionally show up on the SSAT. A neonate is a baby, who grows into a toddler. An adolescent grows into an adult.

5. E – This is an occupation relationship. A biologist's job is to study life. An ecologist's job is to study nature. Don't be fooled by choice A, a forecaster studies meteorology and not astronomy.

Reading section

Reading practice

1. C – Choice A is too broad, the passage is about just one aspect of Aztec culture. The passage mentions other cultures, but that is not the main idea, so choice B is out. The same is true for choice E. There is no mention of the Spanish invaders, so we can rule out choice D. We are left with C, which echoes the last sentence.

2. B – Choice B is correct because the passage specifically tells us that the purpose of the Temazcal is not relaxation.

3. D – The passage is a no-nonsense non-fiction passage. We can assume that the author is interested because he or she chose to write about the subject.

4. A – The first paragraph talks about sweat lodges in other cultures. Immediately after that, the passage reads "The Temazcal, however, are not used for ceremonial purposes or relaxation". The word "however" implies that the sweat lodges in other cultures were used for that purpose.

5. D – The passage tells us that the door faces south and the south is the "pathway of the dead", so I is correct. The passage also says that the pathway of the dead begins with birth, so II is wrong because the door does not represent death only. The passage says that the center of the lodge represents the womb, so the door in must lead there and III is also correct.

Math section

Math practice

1. D – For this one, we need to compare each of the answer choices to a fraction that is equal to $\frac{3}{4}$.

Answer choice	Equal to $\frac{3}{4}$	Which is greater?
(A) $\frac{6}{8}$	$\frac{6}{8}$	Equal
(B) $\frac{10}{12}$	$\frac{9}{12}$	Answer choice
(C) $\frac{18}{23}$	$\frac{18}{24}$	Answer choice
(D) $\frac{26}{36}$	$\frac{27}{36}$	$\frac{3}{4}$
(E) $\frac{33}{44}$	$\frac{33}{44}$	Equal

The only answer choice that is less than $\frac{3}{4}$ is choice D.

2. C – We can use equivalent fractions to set this up.

$$\frac{80}{100} = \frac{x}{20}$$

Now we can cross multiply to solve:

$$20 \times 80 = 100x$$
$$1600 = 100x$$
$$16 = x$$

3. B – For this problem, the builder has to buy more boards than he needs because they only come in packs of 12. 5 bundles would only give him 60 boards, so choice A is out. 6 bundles would give him 72 boards, so choice B is the correct answer.

4. A – Draw this one out. It should look something like this:

In this drawing, the lights are spaced every 20 yards. If you count up the number of lights, there are 22 of them. If you try to do it the math way, it is too easy to double count.

5. A – We can just plug in the answer choices for this one. If we plug in 3 (choice A), we get $3g + 6 = 3(3) + 6 = 9 + 6 = 15$. Since it is equal to 15 and not greater than 15, choice A is the correct answer.

6. E – We need to remember PEMDAS, or order of operations, for this question. Since the P stands for parentheses, we have to do what is in parentheses first:

$$40 - (6^2) \div 9 + 8 = 40 - 36 \div 9 + 8$$

Now it gets a little tricky. It would be very tempting at this point to simply go from left to right. However, we must perform division before we perform subtraction or addition. If we do this, we get:

$$40 - 36 \div 9 + 8 = 40 - 4 + 8 = 36 + 8 = 44$$

7. D – In order to answer this question, we first need to identify that this pattern is an arithmetic sequence. We can tell that it is an arithmetic sequence because the same number is added each day (+3). Now that we know that, we can use the formula $a_n = a_1 + d(n - 1)$ to determine the nth term. In this formula, n refers to the number of the term (first, second, third, etc.), a_n refers to the term itself, and a_1 is the first term, and d is the difference between each term and the next term. We can plug in for the variables with the numbers given in the question and solve:

$$a_n = a_1 + d(n - 1) = 2 + 3(17 - 1) = 50$$

Workout #9

Vocabulary

Roots

Below are some roots. I will give you the definition of each root and then two examples of words that have that root. Look up the meanings of those words and write the definitions in the blanks provided. As you look up the definition of each word, think about how it relates to the root. After you write the definition of each word, write a sentence using the word or a memory trick or association for remembering the word.

Root: *junct*
　　Definition – join
Examples:
　　Adjunct
　　　　Definition:
　　　　Sentence or memory trick:
　　Junction
　　　　Definition:
　　　　Sentence or memory trick:

Root: *greg*
　　Definition – group or to gather
Examples:
　　Gregarious
　　　　Definition:
　　　　Sentence or memory trick:
　　Aggregate
　　　　Definition:
　　　　Sentence or memory trick:

Word to remember!

Rendezvous – a meeting, usually in secret

Example: Romeo and Juliet had a rendezvous that ended very, very badly.

Now, MAKE FLASHCARDS FOR ALL THE WORDS ABOVE – AND STUDY THEM!

Verbal section

Synonyms practice

TIME YOURSELF – THESE QUESTIONS SHOULD TAKE LESS THAN 3 MINUTES.

1. ADJUNCT:
   - (A) projectile
   - (B) associate
   - (C) image
   - (D) sum
   - (E) presentation

2. GREGARIOUS:
   - (A) complaining
   - (B) adequate
   - (C) reluctant
   - (D) social
   - (E) riotous

3. MALICE:
   - (A) hostility
   - (B) infraction
   - (C) diligence
   - (D) reward
   - (E) depletion

4. EUPHEMISTIC:

   (A) general

   (B) blunt

   (C) fundamental

   (D) truthful

   (E) inoffensive

5. FRACTIOUS:

   (A) friendly

   (B) ill

   (C) irritable

   (D) credible

   (E) malevolent

Synonyms strategies checklist

Check off the strategies that you used. If you didn't use any of these strategies, go back and look over your work!

Did you…	Yes	No
1. Use roots to figure out meaning?	____	____
2. Use context?	____	____
3. Use positive or negative?	____	____
4. Rule out what you could and then guess?	____	____

Analogies practice

TIME YOURSELF – THESE QUESTIONS SHOULD TAKE LESS THAN 3 MINUTES.

1. Aggregate is to decentralize as

   (A) credible is to unbelievable

   (B) malevolent is to malicious

   (C) rancorous is to unhappy

   (D) gregarious is to friendly

   (E) magnanimous is to wealthy

2. Influential is to magnate as

   (A) frugal is to banker
   (B) concise is to writer
   (C) tactful is to diplomat
   (D) magnificent is to hill
   (E) eloquent is to farmer

3. Anachronism is to obsolete as

   (A) restaurant is to noisy
   (B) flicker is to roaring
   (C) asset is to useless
   (D) darkness is to dawn
   (E) neophyte is to inexperienced

4. Lift is to person as

   (A) wrench is to plumber
   (B) motor is to truck
   (C) illusion is to fantasy
   (D) jack is to car
   (E) pipe is to water

5. Wave is to tsunami as

   (A) rain is to sunshine
   (B) hill is to mountain
   (C) witness is to lawyer
   (D) negligence is to care
   (E) cover is to book

Analogies strategies checklist

Check off the strategies that you used. If you didn't use any of these strategies, go back and look over your work!

Did you...   Yes   No

1. Identify the relationship if you knew the words?   ____   ____

2. Go to the answer choices and rule out the ones
   that were not related or that couldn't have
   the same relationship as the question words
   if you didn't know the words?   ____   ____

3. Guess if you could rule out even one?   ____   ____

Reading section

Reading practice

Below is a practice reading passage. It is an adapted folktale from England. Folktales are one of the types of passages that you will see on this test.

TIME YOURSELF – THIS PASSAGE AND QUESTIONS SHOULD TAKE A TOTAL OF 5 MINUTES

Carved on one of the pews in the church of Zennor in West Cornwall is a strange figure of a mermaid. Depicted with flowing hair, a mirror in one hand and a comb in the other, the Zennor folk tell a strange story about her.

Line 5
Years and years ago, they say, a beautiful and richly dressed lady used to attend the church sometimes. Nobody knew where she came from, although her unusual beauty and her glorious voice caused her to be the subject of discussion throughout the parish.

So attractive was she that half the young men of the village fell in love with her, and one of them, Mathey Trewella, a handsome youth and one of the best

10
singers in the neighbourhood, determined that he would discover who she was.

The beautiful stranger had smiled at him in church one Sunday, and after service he followed her as she walked away towards the cliffs.

Mathey Trewella never returned to Zennor, nor did the lovely stranger ever attend church again.

15
Years passed by, and Mathey's strange disappearance was almost forgotten when, one Sunday morning, a ship cast anchor off Pendower Cove, near Zennor. The captain of the vessel was sitting idling on the deck when he heard a beautiful voice hailing him from the sea. Looking over the side he saw the mermaid, her long yellow hair floating all around her.

20
She asked him to be so kind as to pull up his anchor, for it was resting upon the doorway of her house under the sea and she was anxious to get back to Mathey, her husband, and her children.

In alarm, the captain weighed anchor and stood out to sea, for sailors fear that mermaids will bring bad luck. But later he returned and told the Zennor folk

25
of Mathey's fate, and they, to commemorate the strange event, and to warn other young men against the wiles of the merrymaids, had the mermaid figure carved in the church.

And there it is today for all the world to see, and to prove, to those who do not believe the old stories, the truth of poor Mathey Trewella's sad fate.

1. According to the passage, Mathey Trewella was

   (A) a merman
   (B) a farmer
   (C) a good singer
   (D) an older gentleman
   (E) a sailor

2. The people of the village had a figure of a mermaid carved into their church in order to

   (A) celebrate Mathey Trewella's life
   (B) caution other youths against the charms of mermaids
   (C) remember the beautiful female singer that had once visited their church
   (D) advise against gossiping about other women in church
   (E) commemorate the captain who was smart enough to stay away from the mermaid

3. This passage would most likely be found

   (A) in a newspaper account
   (B) in a novel
   (C) on a radio address
   (D) in a textbook
   (E) in an anthology of traditional tales

4. All of the following words can be used to describe the mermaid EXCEPT:

   (A) cunning
   (B) beautiful
   (C) wily
   (D) cautious
   (E) bold

5. A good title for this passage would be

   (A) The Importance of Avoiding Mermaids
   (B) How Mermaids Trick Ship Captains
   (C) The Grief of Mathey Trewella's Family
   (D) Watch Out for Women Who Can Sing
   (E) Immigration to the Village of Zennor

Reading strategies checklist

Check off the strategies that you used. If you didn't use any of these strategies, go back and look over your work!

Did you...   Yes   No

1. Mark "S" and "G"?   ____   ____

2. Reread the last sentences before answering
   general questions?   ____   ____

3. Underline the answers in the passage
   for specific questions?   ____   ____

Math section

Math practice

TIME YOURSELF – THESE PROBLEMS SHOULD TAKE YOU ABOUT 9 MINUTES TOTAL

1. $1\frac{3}{5} + 4\frac{4}{5} + 3\frac{2}{5} =$

   (A) 8.8
   (B) 9.25
   (C) 9.5
   (D) 9.8
   (E) 10.125

2. All of the following are equal except

   (A) $3 \times \frac{5}{6}$

   (B) $6 \times \frac{5}{12}$

   (C) $9 \times \frac{15}{18}$

   (D) $12 \times \frac{5}{24}$

   (E) $15 \times \frac{1}{6}$

3. Ms. Smith wants to cover her lawn in sod. Her yard is 81 square yards. The sod is sold in square feet. How many square feet of sod will she need?

    (A) 27
    (B) 81
    (C) 243
    (D) 540
    (E) 729

4. Molly has a savings account that earns 6% interest in a year. If she started the account one year ago with $7,500 and has not made any deposits since, how much money does she now have in her account?

    (A) $450
    (B) $7,950
    (C) $8,200
    (D) $8,250
    (E) $8,325

5. Seventeen students are on a fieldtrip to the zoo and they all want to see either the lions or the bears. Fourteen children want to see the lions and eleven students want to see the bears. How many students want to see both the lions and the bears?

    (A) 8
    (B) 9
    (C) 11
    (D) 17
    (E) 25

6. Simplify: $\dfrac{8a^5b^2c}{2b^3c^4} \times \dfrac{ac^3}{4a^2b^2}$

    (A) $\dfrac{a}{b}$

    (B) $\dfrac{a^4}{b^3}$

    (C) $\dfrac{2a^4}{b^3}$

    (D) $\dfrac{2a^4}{b^2}$

    (E) $\dfrac{4a^4c}{b^3}$

7. There are green and blue pens in a jar. If the ratio of blue pens to green pens is 2 to 3, which could be the total number of pens in the jar?

   (A) 8
   (B) 9
   (C) 12
   (D) 18
   (E) 25

Vocabulary

Look them up!

Verbal section

Synonyms practice

1. B – The "ad" suffix means to or towards and the "junct" root means to join, so we are looking for something that roughly means joining to. An associate is someone who is connected, so that is the correct answer.

2. D – The "greg" root means group or gather, so we are looking for a word related to getting together. If someone is social, they like to get together with other people, so choice D is correct.

3. A – The "mal" root means bad. We are looking for a word that is very negative. Choices C and D are positive, so we can rule those out. An infraction occurs when a rule is broken and depletion is the using up of resources. While both of these are negative, they don't capture the really bad nature of the "mal" root. Hostility does so choice A is correct.

4. E – The "eu" root means well or good, so we are looking for something positive. Choices A-D are either neutral or could be good or bad. Inoffensive is a positive word in that it means not upsetting anyone. Choice E is correct.

5. C – The root "frac" is negative, but not overly so. We can rule out choices A and D because they are positive. Choice E, malevolent, means purely evil, which is too strong for the "frac" root. We are down to ill or irritable. To be fractious is to be irritable, or really grumpy.

Analogies practice

1. A – Aggregate and decentralize are antonyms. Aggregate is to combine together and decentralize is to spread out. Choices B and D are synonyms, so we can rule those out. Choices C and E have words that are unrelated, so we can also rule those out. If we use roots, it is easy to see that credible and unbelievable are antonyms, so choice A is correct.

2. C – Influential is a characteristic of a magnate (a magnate is a powerful business leader). The words in choice E are unrelated, so we can rule that out. If you look at choices A, B, and D, there is not a strong relationship. A banker could be frugal, a writer could be concise, and a hill could be magnificent, but the word "could" tells us that we can rule out these choices. We are left with choice C, and tactful is a characteristic of a diplomat.

3. E – This one is a characteristic relationship as well, but we have to flip the words. Obsolete is a characteristic of an anachronism (something that is out of date). We now have to remember to flip the words in the answer choices when we plug in. Choice E is correct because inexperienced is a characteristic of a neophyte (did you recognize the "neo" root that means new? A neophyte is a beginner.) Don't be fooled by choice A. A restaurant could be noisy, but doesn't have to be.

4. D – This is a used for relationship. A lift is used to lift a person (a lift is another word for an elevator). A jack is used to lift a car, so choice D is correct. The word "lift" has more than one meaning. Its most common meaning is a verb, but if we look at the answer choices, we can see that all of the first words are nouns. That tells us that lift must have a noun meaning in this analogy.

5. B – This is a degree relationship. A really big wave is a tsunami. A really big hill is a mountain, so choice B is correct.

Reading section

Reading practice

1. C – The only answer that has evidence in the passage is that Mathey Trewella was a good singer. In the third paragraph, the passage states that Mathey Trewella was "one of the best singers in the neighbourhood."

2. B – In lines 25-26, we are told that the carved figure was created "to warn other young men against the wiles of the merrymaids." Choice B most closely restates this.

3. E – This is a folktale, so it would most likely be found in an anthology (a collection) of traditional tales (also called folktales).

4. D – There is evidence for all of the adjectives except cautious. She was very daring, so cautious is out.

5. A – Choices B and C are mentioned in the passage, but are not the main idea. Choice D is too general – the passage warns us about mermaids who sing, not women in general. Choice E is way too broad – the passage is not talking about immigration to the village in general. Choice A best matches the last sentence of the passage.

Math section

Math practice

1. D – Let's use grouping to solve this one.

$$1\frac{3}{5} + 4\frac{4}{5} + 3\frac{2}{5} =$$

$$1 + \frac{3}{5} + 4 + \frac{4}{5} + 3 + \frac{2}{5} =$$

$$1 + 4 + 3 + \frac{3}{5} + \frac{2}{5} + \frac{4}{5} =$$

$$8 + \frac{5}{5} + \frac{4}{5} =$$

$$8 + 1 + \frac{4}{5} = 9\frac{4}{5}$$

9.8 is equal to $9\frac{4}{5}$, so choice D is correct.

2. C – If we cross cancel, we get that choices A, B, D, and E are all equal to $\frac{5}{2}$. Choice C equals $\frac{15}{2}$, so that is the correct answer.

3. E – The trick to this question is that the requirements are given in square yards, but the sod comes in square feet. Since the lawn is 81 square yards, let's assume that it is 9 yards by 9 yards. If we convert this into feet (by multiplying by 3), we get that the yard is 27 feet by 27 feet. To find the square footage, we have to multiply 27 by 27. Since we don't have a calculator, let's find a range. If it was 20 feet by 20 feet, that would be 400 square feet. If it was 30 feet by 30 feet, that would be 900 square feet. Since 27 is closer to 30 than to 20, we want an answer choice that is closer to 900 than 400. Choice E is correct.

4. B – We can estimate for this problem. It is easy to find 5%, and that is close to 6%. We first find 10% by moving the decimal one place to the left to get $750. 5% is half of that, or $375. When we add that to her original balance, we get $7,875. Since the interest was 6% and not 5%, we want an answer that is just a little more than $7,875, so choice B is correct.

5. A – If we add 14 and 11, we get 25. However, there are only 17 students. This tells us that $25 - 17$, or 8, students want to see both the lions and the bears.

6. B – The easiest way to answer this question is to use the commutative property of multiplication to put like terms together. If we do this, we get:

$$\frac{8a^5b^2c}{2b^3c^4} \times \frac{ac^3}{4a^2b^2} = \frac{8 \times a^5 \times a \times b^2 \times c \times c^3}{2 \times 4 \times a^2 \times b^3 \times b^2 \times c^4}$$

Now we can combine like terms:

$$\frac{8 \times a^5 \times a \times b^2 \times c \times c^3}{2 \times 4 \times a^2 \times b^3 \times b^2 \times c^4} = \frac{8 \times a^6 \times b^2 \times c^4}{8 \times a^2 \times b^5 \times c^4}$$

This makes it easy to see that if we cancel out, we are left with $\frac{a^4}{b^3}$.

7. E – The trick to this type of question is that we have to turn the ratio, which is part to part, into fractions, which are part to whole. If there are 2 blue pens for every 3 green pens, then $\frac{2}{5}$ of the pens are blue and $\frac{3}{5}$ of the pens are green. Now we can see that the total number of pens has to be divisible by 5 since we can't have a partial pen. Only answer choice E is evenly divisible by 5.

Vocabulary

Roots

Below are some roots. I will give you the definition of each root and then two examples of words that have that root. Look up the meanings of those words and write the definitions in the blanks provided. As you look up the definition of each word, think about how it relates to the root. After you write the definition of each word, write a sentence using the word or a memory trick or association for remembering the word.

Root: *doc*
Definition – to teach
Examples:
Doctrine
Definition:
Sentence or memory trick:
Docile
Definition:
Sentence or memory trick:

Root: *mis / mit*
Definition – to send
Examples:
Transmit
Definition:
Sentence or memory trick:
Remit
Definition:
Sentence or memory trick:

Word to remember!

Adept – skilled

Example: He was quite an adept video game player. He often reached the last level quickly.

Now, MAKE FLASHCARDS FOR ALL THE WORDS ABOVE – AND STUDY THEM!

Verbal section

Synonyms practice

TIME YOURSELF – THESE QUESTIONS SHOULD TAKE ABOUT 3 MINUTES.

1. DISMISS:

    (A) dehydrate
    (B) protect
    (C) discard
    (D) encourage
    (E) equate

2. JUNCTURE:

    (A) joining
    (B) scruples
    (C) vacuum
    (D) incision
    (E) neologism

3. RENDEZVOUS:

    (A) battle
    (B) meeting
    (C) forwardness
    (D) agent
    (E) crook

4. DOCILE:

   (A) mundane

   (B) strong

   (C) public

   (D) agreeable

   (E) common

5. REFRACTORY:

   (A) profound

   (B) gregarious

   (C) deflated

   (D) beneficial

   (E) difficult

Synonyms strategies checklist

Check off the strategies that you used. If you didn't use any of these strategies, go back and look over your work!

Did you...   Yes   No

   1. Use roots to figure out meaning?   ____   ____

   2. Use context?   ____   ____

   3. Use positive or negative?   ____   ____

   4. Rule out what you could and then guess?   ____   ____

Analogies practice

TIME YOURSELF – THESE QUESTIONS SHOULD TAKE LESS THAN 3 MINUTES.

1. Indoctrinate is to brainwash as

   (A) eulogize is to praise

   (B) expedite is to delay

   (C) run is to tire

   (D) encourage is to provoke

   (E) maintain is to abandon

2. Submit is to revoke as

   (A) accomplish is to climb
   (B) create is to schedule
   (C) excise is to cut
   (D) debase is to devalue
   (E) ascend is to descend

3. Novel is to invention as

   (A) solid is to square
   (B) quaint is to city
   (C) unified is to aggregation
   (D) detrimental is to progress
   (E) found is to object

4. Missile is to rocket scientist as

   (A) car is to owner
   (B) plant is to agronomist
   (C) beach is to factory worker
   (D) teacher is to principal
   (E) chorus is to director

5. Cup is to pint as

   (A) week is to day
   (B) liter is to gallon
   (C) plate is to platter
   (D) pint is to quart
   (E) chapter is to book

Analogies strategies checklist

Check off the strategies that you used. If you didn't use any of these strategies, go back and look over your work!

Did you...   Yes   No

1. Identify the relationship if you knew the words?   ____   ____

2. Go to the answer choices and rule out the ones
    that were not related or that couldn't have
    the same relationship as the question words
    if you didn't know the words?   ____   ____

3. Guess if you could rule out even one?   ____   ____

Reading section

Reading practice

Below is a practice reading passage. It is a primary document written by C.J. Arthur during the First World War. Primary documents are one of the types of passages that you will see on this test.

TIME YOURSELF – THIS PASSAGE AND QUESTIONS SHOULD TAKE A TOTAL OF 5 MINUTES

I was born in November 1898 so that when war was declared I was at school. I joined the School Cadet Battalion in 1914 and was appointed corporal.

At Whitsun, 1915, I told the O.C. cadet I was going to join up. "Good," he said. "How old do you want to be?"

Line 5   We fixed things between us, and armed with a letter from him, I presented myself, after attestation, to the colonel of an infantry battalion which was just being formed, and on the strength of the letter I was appointed a lance-corporal and told to get my hair cut.

I did so and afterwards saw the regimental sergeant-major, who put me 10   through my paces and told me to get my hair cut. In ten weeks I had been made sergeant.

We did the usual training in England until May 1916, then went to France as a complete division. Some of the N.C.O.'s were sent up the line for instruction with a Scottish battalion at Ploegsteert. What a lovely war that was!

15   In complete daylight we marched up to and through the wood to find a network of trenches and sand-bags. Still in daylight, but now through the trenches, one was able to wander up to the front line.

During instruction with the Scottish, I was sent out on a wiring party. We were subjected to machine-gun fire, but oh, blissful ignorance, I kept upright, a 20   perfectly good 6 feet of human target!

"Git doon, ye fool!" and, crash! my legs were knocked from under me and I fell flat on my face with a good coil of barbed wire in my stomach. The Scot explained and marvelled at my ignorance.

1. This passage is most likely to be found

(A) in a newspaper
(B) in an encyclopedia
(C) in a research report
(D) in a diary
(E) on a propaganda poster

2. Why does the author say "what a lovely war that was" in line 14?

   (A) He had not yet seen combat.
   (B) The weather was nice on that day.
   (C) His battalion was winning the battle.
   (D) He was with his friends from home.
   (E) He had not yet received a promotion.

3. It can be inferred from the passage that

   (A) the author joined the army after graduating from high school
   (B) the author was old enough to serve in the army
   (C) the author lied about his age in order to serve in the army
   (D) the regimental sergeant-major knew how old the author really was
   (E) there was no age requirement for the army

4. The author's tone can best be described as

   (A) hostile
   (B) conversational
   (C) scholarly
   (D) persuasive
   (E) nervous

5. What does the author mean by "blissful ignorance" in line 19?

   (A) It is good to be uninformed.
   (B) He is happy to be at war.
   (C) He is happy to have been promoted to sergeant.
   (D) Lacking education can sometimes be an advantage.
   (E) He is glad that he did not know how much danger he was really in at the time.

6. A good title for this passage would be

   (A) A History of the First World War
   (B) Soldiers Go To Battle
   (C) A Young Man's Story of Going to War
   (D) Changes for Men in World War I
   (E) Weaponry in the First World War

Reading strategies checklist

Check off the strategies that you used. If you didn't use any of these strategies, go back and look over your work!

Did you…   Yes   No

1. Mark "S" and "G"?   ____   ____

2. Reread the last sentences before answering
   general questions?   ____   ____

3. Underline the answers in the passage
   for specific questions?   ____   ____

Math section

Math practice

TIME YOURSELF – THESE PROBLEMS SHOULD TAKE YOU ABOUT 9 MINUTES TOTAL

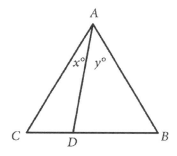

1. In the figure above, triangle ABC is an equilateral triangle, meaning that all the sides are the same length. If $2x = y$, then what is the measure of x?

   (A) 15
   (B) 20
   (C) 30
   (D) 45
   (E) 60

2. There are five students in a class. Adam is older than Bruce. Josh is older than Adam. Kara is younger than Adam. Sam is older than Kara. Who is oldest student in the class?

(A) Josh

(B) Adam

(C) Sam

(D) Bruce

(E) It cannot be determined from information given

3. If three numbers add to 36, which of the following must be true?

(A) All of the numbers are positive

(B) None of the numbers are greater than 36

(C) The average of the numbers is 12

(D) All of the numbers are even

(E) All of the numbers are odd

4. In a store, some boxes have two light bulbs and some boxes have three light bulbs. There are the same number of each of these boxes. If there are a total of 15 light bulbs, how many boxes have three light bulbs in them?

(A) 7

(B) 6

(C) 5

(D) 4

(E) 3

5. Which of the following has exactly two lines of symmetry?

(A)

(B)

(C)

(D)

(E)

6. In a bag there are red, green, and yellow marbles. The ratio of red to green to yellow marbles is $2:3:5$. If there are a total of 40 marbles in the bag, how many of them are green?

(A) 3
(B) 8
(C) 10
(D) 12
(E) 20

7. Alexandra is doing chores to earn extra money. On the first day she earned $1. On the second day, she earned $2, and on the third day she earned $3. If this pattern continues, how much money will she have earned at the end of the thirtieth day?

(A) $30
(B) $320
(C) $465
(D) $524
(E) $930

Workout #10 Answers

Vocabulary

Look them up!

Verbal section

Synonyms practice

1. C – Did you notice that dismiss and discard have the same root? That is a good clue that discard is the right answer.

2. A – The root "junct" means to join, so a juncture is a joining.

3. B – This is a word to remember from Workout #9, so make sure you have a flashcard for rendezvous if you missed this one.

4. D – If someone is docile, that person goes with the flow. This is a stretch from the "doc" root meaning to teach, but the English language can be a quirky beast.

5. E – The "re" root means again or back and "fract" means to break, so we know refractory must be something negative. That lets us rule out profound, gregarious, and beneficial (A, B, and D). If a person is refractory, she just likes to be difficult.

Analogies practice

1. A – This is a synonyms relationship. To indoctrinate a person is to brainwash, or make a person believe that one way of thinking is the absolute truth. To eulogize is to praise, so choice A is correct.

2. E – This is an antonym relationship. To submit something is to give it to someone, but to revoke something is to take it away. Choices A and B are unrelated and choices C and D are synonyms. We can tell from the roots in choice E that ascend and descend are antonyms.

3. C – Novel is a characteristic of an invention. (Did you see the "nov" root that means new?) Choices A, D, and E are unrelated. A city could be quaint, but it isn't always, so choice B is out. Unified is a characteristic of an aggregation, however, so choice C is correct.

4. B – This is an occupation relationship. Working with missiles is the job of a rocket scientist. Working with plants is the job of an agronomist. (Do you see the "agr" root, the same one that is in agriculture?)

5. D – There are two cups in a pint. There are also two pints in a quart, so choice D is correct. Choice B is tempting because liter and gallon are also units that measure volume, but liter is from the metric system and gallon is from the English system.

Reading section

Reading practice

1. D – The tone of the passage is very personal and tells a story. The passage also uses the first person (or the word "I"). A diary best fits the tone of the passage so choice D is correct.

2. A – The speaker talks about how he marched through the woods not yet knowing he could get shot at, so the fact that he had not yet seen combat led him to say that it was a lovely war. There is not evidence for the other answer choices.

3. C – The passage tells us that the O.C. cadet asked him, "How old you do you want to be?", which implies that the author and the cadet were making up an age for him, or lying about his age.

4. B – The author writes in the first person and includes dialogue that makes it seem like he is just telling a story. This makes the tone conversational.

5. E – The author describes walking upright even though there was machine gun fire, implying that it didn't occur to him that he could get hit. Choice E best captures this situation where the phrase "blissful ignorance" was used.

6. C – Choices A, B, D, and E are way too broad for this passage. Choice C goes with the very personal story that is in the passage.

Math section

Math practice

1. B – The problem tells us that the triangle is equilateral. That means that the sides are all equal, and it also means that all of the angles of triangle ABC are 60 degrees. That tells us that $x + y = 60$. We also know that $2x = y$. If we plug in answer choice C, then x is 30 and y is 60. This adds up to more than 60 degrees, so we know that x must be

smaller. If we plug in choice B, we get that x is 20 and therefore y is 40. Together, these add up to 60 degrees, so we know that choice B is correct.

2. E – We can figure out that Josh is older than Adam who is older than Bruce and Kara. We also know that Sam must be older than Kara, but we have no other comparison for Sam. Sam could be older than Josh or he could be younger than Josh and still be older than Kara. Therefore, there is no way to tell who is oldest.

3. C – Let's try each of the answer choices. For choice A we can plug in 40, 2, and −6 and still get 36 as a sum, so we know that the numbers don't all have to be positive and choice A is out. These same numbers also allow us to rule out choice B, since 40 is greater than 36. If we look at choice C and think about what an average is, we know that choice C must be correct. To find an average, we divide the sum by the number of numbers. The problem tells us that the sum is 36 and there are 3 numbers. Since $36 \div 3 = 12$, the average must be 12.

4. E – We can plug in answer choices to solve this one. We will start with choice C. If we have 5 boxes of three bulbs each, that alone gives 15 light bulbs. Since we have a total of 15 light bulbs, we know that choice C is too big and we should go smaller. If we plug in choice D, having 4 boxes of three light bulbs gives us 12 light bulbs. The problem says that there is an equal number of boxes that have two light bulbs. That gives us 4 boxes of two bulbs each, or 8 light bulbs. If we add 12 and 8 together we get a total of 20 bulbs, which is too many. If we plug in choice E, we get that there are 9 bulbs from 3 boxes of three and 6 bulbs from 3 boxes of two, and that adds up to a total of 15 bulbs. Choice E is correct.

5. B – Choice A is a circle, which has infinite lines of symmetry, so choice A is out. Choice B has two lines of symmetry since it is an oval (go ahead and draw the two lines to prove it to yourself). Choice C has four lines of symmetry (don't forget to include the diagonals). Choice D has five lines of symmetry and choice E has only one. Only choice B works.

6. D – The first step is turn the ratio into fractions. Since the ratio is part to part to part, we have to add those parts together to get the total, which is the denominator in our fractions. Since there are a total of 10 parts and 3 of those parts are green, we know that $\frac{3}{10}$ of the marbles are green. Since "of" tells us to multiply, we can do $\frac{3}{10} \times 40$ since there are 40 marbles, and get that there must be 12 green marbles.

7. C – The key to this question is to recognize that it is asking for the sum of a sequence and not just the thirtieth term. To find the sum of a sequence, we use the formula:

$$s_n = \frac{n(a_1 + a_n)}{2}$$

In this formula, s_n represents the sum of a sequence with n terms. The term a_1 represents the first terms in the sequence and a_n represents the last term in the sequence. Now we have to plug in what we are given. We are looking for the sum of the first 30 terms, so $n = 30$. The first term is 1 so $a_1 = 1$ and in this case the value of the term is the same as the number of the term so $a_n = 30$.

When we plug in those values, we get:

$$s_n = \frac{n(a_1 + a_n)}{2} = \frac{30(1 + 30)}{2} = 465$$

Vocabulary

Roots

Below are some roots. I will give you the definition of each root and then two examples of words that have that root. Look up the meanings of those words and write the definitions in the blanks provided. As you look up the definition of each word, think about how it relates to the root. After you write the definition of each word, write a sentence using the word or a memory trick or association for remembering the word.

Root: *ques / quer / quis*
Definition – ask or seek
Examples:
Inquisitive
Definition:
Sentence or memory trick:
Query
Definition:
Sentence or memory trick:

Root: *vac*
Definition – empty
Examples:
Vacuum
Definition:
Sentence or memory trick:
Vacate
Definition:
Sentence or memory trick:

Word to remember!

Meticulous – paying close attention to detail
Example: She was quite meticulous and never left a mess behind.

Now, MAKE FLASHCARDS FOR ALL THE WORDS ABOVE – AND STUDY THEM!

Verbal section

Synonyms practice

TIME YOURSELF – THESE QUESTIONS SHOULD TAKE ABOUT 3 MINUTES.

1. QUERY:

    (A) impact
    (B) ease
    (C) pledge
    (D) question
    (E) claim

2. CONGREGATION:

    (A) argument
    (B) assembly
    (C) reduction
    (D) vacuum
    (E) deterrent

3. EVACUATE:

    (A) preclude
    (B) detour
    (C) innovate
    (D) indoctrinate
    (E) empty

4. METICULOUS:

   (A) strict
   (B) fun
   (C) frugal
   (D) adept
   (E) united

5. NOVELTY:

   (A) malice
   (B) content
   (C) newness
   (D) magnate
   (E) doctrine

Analogies practice

TIME YOURSELF – THESE QUESTIONS SHOULD TAKE LESS THAN 3 MINUTES.

1. Inquisitive is to investigator as

   (A) funny is to teacher
   (B) scholarly is to professor
   (C) scary is to holiday
   (D) confident is to actor
   (E) concise is to writer

2. Segregate is to aggregate as

   (A) combine is to join
   (B) favor is to cross
   (C) request is to submit
   (D) deplete is to increase
   (E) describe is to eulogize

3. Malign is to praise as

    (A) welcome is to reject
    (B) benefit is to accomplish
    (C) excise is to encourage
    (D) malfunction is to fracture
    (E) innovate is to revolutionize

4. Journalist is to chronicle as

    (A) biologist is to lecture
    (B) plumber is to build
    (C) doctor is to treat
    (D) dentist is to encourage
    (E) editor is to write

5. Probable is to definite as likely is to

    (A) possible
    (B) denied
    (C) discouraged
    (D) undecided
    (E) certain

Reading section

Reading practice

Below is a practice reading passage. It is a biography of an artist – one of the types of passages that you will see on this test.

TIME YOURSELF – THIS PASSAGE AND QUESTIONS SHOULD TAKE A TOTAL OF 5 MINUTES

Vincent Van Gogh was a brilliant but troubled artist who found acclaim only after his tragic death. He was born in 1853 in Groot-Zundert, Holland. From an early age, he was very emotional and lacking in self-confidence. After a series of unsuccessful occupations, he went to study art in Belgium. His goal was to bring
Line 5 happiness to others by creating beauty, even if happiness seemed to elude him. In Belgium, he found a community of artists that he could develop his talents with. One of these artists was Paul Gauguin. They had a close relationship, until 1888, when Van Gogh went after Gauguin with a razor blade during an argument. Gauguin was able to defend himself, but in the exchange, Van Gogh cut off part of
10 his own earlobe. After this, Van Gogh alternated between periods of insanity and immense creativity. He was sent to an asylum and later went to live with Dr. Gachet, who could keep an eye on him. Just a couple of months after that, he was dead by his own hand. The man whom we now consider a genius sold just one painting during his career. In 1990, however, a portrait he painted of Dr. Gachet
15 sold for $82.5 million.

1. This author would most likely agree that Van Gogh

    (A) lived a long time
    (B) did not find fame during his lifetime
    (C) was never a good friend
    (D) was harmed by being bullied as a child
    (E) relied too heavily upon Dr. Gachet

2. When discussing Van Gogh, the author's tone can best be described as

    (A) cheery
    (B) agitated
    (C) objective
    (D) inquisitive
    (E) furious

3. Which of the following questions is answered in the passage?

   (A) How many paintings did Van Gogh sell in his lifetime?
   (B) What did other artists think of Van Gogh?
   (C) In what town did he die?
   (D) Who were his parents?
   (E) What was the subject of most of his paintings?

4. This passage deals primarily with

   (A) Van Gogh's paintings
   (B) impressionist artists
   (C) Van Gogh's childhood
   (D) Van Gogh's various careers
   (E) the mental health of Van Gogh

5. When the author writes, "happiness seemed to elude him" (line 5), it means

   (A) Van Gogh did not want to be happy
   (B) Van Gogh was happy for a time
   (C) Van Gogh didn't seem able to achieve happiness
   (D) Van Gogh lived in uncertain times
   (E) Van Gogh's family was concerned about him

Math section

Math practice

TIME YOURSELF – THESE PROBLEMS SHOULD TAKE YOU ABOUT 9 MINUTES TOTAL

1. If the sides in the figure above are all 5 units long, what is the perimeter of this figure?

    (A) 20
    (B) 22
    (C) 25
    (D) 30
    (E) 32

2. A cake was cut into 24 pieces and evenly distributed among the party guests. Which could NOT be the total number of guests?

    (A) 2
    (B) 3
    (C) 7
    (D) 8
    (E) 12

Questions 3 and 4 refer to the following graph.

3. How many more cars were sold in May than in April?

   (A) 2
   (B) 200
   (C) 300
   (D) 400
   (E) 1000

4. The number of cars sold in March is how many times the number of cars sold in February?

   (A) 2
   (B) 3
   (C) 5
   (D) 350
   (E) 700

5. A tennis player gets her serve in 80% of the time. In a particular game, her serve went in 20 times. How many times did it land out of bounds?

   (A) 5
   (B) 6
   (C) 7
   (D) 8
   (E) 10

6. Evaluate: $319.896 \div 29.62$

   (A) 1.08
   (B) 10.8
   (C) 100.8
   (D) 120.54
   (E) 180.69

7. Use the number line below to answer the question

   Which point would represent $-\frac{4}{3}$?

   (A) A
   (B) B
   (C) C
   (D) D
   (E) E

Workout #11 Answers

Vocabulary

Look them up!

Verbal section

Synonyms practice

1. D – The "quer" root means to ask or to seek. Choice D, question, comes closest to this meaning.

2. B – The "greg" root means to gather. Choice B, assembly, comes closest to this meaning.

3. E – The root "vac" means to empty, so to evacuate is to empty.

4. A – This is a word to remember from this workout. Please make a flashcard if you have not already.

5. C – The "nov" root means new, so novelty is the newness of something.

Analogies practice

1. B – Inquisitive is a characteristic of an investigator by definition since an investigator's job is to ask questions. Scholarly is a characteristic of a professor since it is a professor's job to be a scholar. A teacher may be funny, an actor may be confident, and a writer could be concise, but these relationships are not strong enough.

2. D – Segregate and aggregate are antonyms. Deplete and increase are also antonyms. If you didn't know what deplete means, you could use roots to figure it out. To complete is to fill something up, but "de" is a negative root, so deplete is to use something up.

3. A – Malign and praise are opposites. To malign something is to say something bad about it, to praise it is the opposite. To welcome someone is the opposite of rejecting that person, so choice A is correct.

4. C – This is an occupation relationship. It is a journalist's job to chronicle, or record, our times. It is also a doctor's job to treat. You may have been tempted by choice E, but it is an editor's job to fix what other people have written, not to write themselves.

5. E – This is a degree relationship. Probable means that something looks like it will happen, but definite is more extreme. Certain is also more extreme than likely.

Reading section

Reading practice

1. B – The passage says that Van Gogh sold only one painting in his lifetime, which is evidence that he did not find fame in his lifetime.

2. C – This is a nonfiction passage, so the tone is objective. Objective means to just give the facts without taking sides, which is a good description for this nonfiction passage.

3. A – Choice A is clearly answered in the second to last sentence. Choice B might be tempting since we know that he did get into a fight with another artist, but choice B refers to artists in the plural, or more than one artist.

4. E – This is one of the rare passages in which the last sentence does not give us the main idea. However, since most of the passage talks about Van Gogh's history with insane asylums and his random attacks, it is safe to say that the main idea is his mental health.

5. C – Elude means to get away. Choices D and E have nothing to do with happiness getting away. There is not evidence that Van Gogh didn't want to be happy or that he was happy for a time, so choices A and B are out. Choice C comes closest in meaning to the idea of happiness eluding, or getting away from, Van Gogh.

Math section

Math practice

1. C – There are five sides to the figure. Each side is 5 units long. To get the perimeter we multiply $5 \times 5 = 25$, or choice C.

2. C – The problem tells us that the cake was evenly distributed. This means that the number of guests must go into 24 evenly. 7 does not go into 24 without a remainder, so that could not be the total number of guests.

3. D – In May, 800 cars were sold, and in April there were 400 cards sold. The difference between these two numbers is 400, so choice D is correct.

4. A – The tricky thing about this problem is that the previous problem asked for the difference in the number of cars sold, so you have that in your head. However, this question asks for how many times, not the difference. There were about 350 cars sold in February and 700 cars sold in March, so there were 2 times as many cars sold in March as in February.

5. A – For this problem, we can set up equivalent fractions.

$$\frac{80}{100} = \frac{20}{x}$$

If we cross-multiply, we get:

$$80x = 2000$$

When we do the math, we get that $x = 25$. That tells us that she served a total of 25 times. Since we know that she got her serve in 20 times, she must have missed 5 times, or choice A.

6. B – This would be a very ugly calculation to do. However, if we look at the answer choices, we can see that they are pretty well spread out. Let's go ahead and do some estimating instead:

$$\frac{319.896}{29.62} \approx \frac{300}{30} \approx 10$$

We can see that our answer should be around 10, and only answer choice B comes close.

7. A – The first step in this problem is to turn our improper fraction into a mixed number so that we can compare it to the numbers on the number line:

$$-\frac{4}{3} = -\left(\frac{3}{3} + \frac{1}{3}\right) = -1\frac{1}{3}$$

Now we can see that we are looking for a point between $-1\frac{1}{2}$ and -1, so choice A is the answer.

Workout #12

Vocabulary

Roots

This is a vocabulary review. Be sure to study the meanings of the roots we have covered before you attempt this section.

Roots review – Next to each root below, write the meaning.

1. *de* _____

2. *cis* _____

3. *fid* _____

4. *pan* _____

5. *loc / loq / log* _____

6. *magna* _____

7. *bene* _____

8. *chron* _____

9. *cred* _____

10. *mal* _____

11. *eu* _____

12. *neo / nov* _____

13. *bio* _____

14. *fract* _____

15. *junct* _____

16. *greg* _____

17. *doc* _____

18. *mis / mit* _____

19. *ques / quer / quis* _____

20. *vac* _____

Verbal section

Synonyms practice

TIME YOURSELF – THESE QUESTIONS SHOULD TAKE ABOUT 3 MINUTES.

1. RANCOROUS:

    (A) wary
    (B) confused
    (C) hostile
    (D) calm
    (E) inquisitive

2. CONGEAL:

    (A) stop
    (B) coagulate
    (C) force
    (D) vacuum
    (E) devalue

3. METICULOUS:

    (A) scrupulous
    (B) unhappy
    (C) stable
    (D) querulous
    (E) funky

4. ADEPT:

    (A) strong
    (B) brilliant
    (C) painstaking
    (D) sporadic
    (E) expert

5. EXACERBATE:

  (A) drive
  (B) corrode
  (C) fancy
  (D) worsen
  (E) strive

Analogies practice

TIME YOURSELF – THESE QUESTIONS SHOULD TAKE LESS THAN 3 MINUTES.

1. Tactful is to offensive as

  (A) obedient is to proper
  (B) proud is to dismayed
  (C) dim is to dull
  (D) practiced is to accomplished
  (E) concise is to serious

2. Obsolete is to phonograph as

  (A) athletic is to marathoner
  (B) cranky is to child
  (C) warm is to ocean
  (D) rancorous is to friendship
  (E) frugal is to vacation

3. Door is to house as

  (A) window is to wall
  (B) stairway is to basement
  (C) hatch is to submarine
  (D) hinge is to shutter
  (E) roof is to mansion

4. Prologue is to epilogue as

   (A) chapter is to book
   (B) words are to sentence
   (C) climax is to ending
   (D) introduction is to conclusion
   (E) author is to editor

5. Euphoria is to malaise as

   (A) fact is to confirmation
   (B) woe is to sadness
   (C) fortune is to wealth
   (D) intelligence is to adeptness
   (E) precision is to error

Reading section

Reading practice

Below is a practice reading passage. It is a poem – one of the types of passages that you will see on this test.

TIME YOURSELF – THIS PASSAGE AND QUESTIONS SHOULD TAKE A TOTAL OF 5 MINUTES

THE TREE

Green stood the Tree,
With its leaves tender bright.
Line 5 "Shall I take them?" said Frost,
As he breathed thro' the night.
"Oh! pray let them be,
Till my blossoms you see!"
Begged the Tree, as she shivered
10 And shook in affright.

Sweet sang the birds
The fair blossoms among.
"Shall I take them?" said Wind,
15 As he swayed them and swung.
"Oh! pray let them be,
Till my berries you see!"
Begged the Tree, as its branches
All quivering hung.
20

Bright grew the berries
Beneath the sun's heat.
"Shall I take them?" said Lassie
So young and so sweet.
25 "Ah! take them, I crave!
Take all that I have!"
Begged the Tree, as it bent
Its full boughs to her feet.

1. During the course of this poem, which of the following happens?

> I. The tree dies
> II. The seasons change
> III. The birds leave the tree

(A) I only
(B) II only
(C) III only
(D) I and II
(E) II and III

2. Why does the tree beg the girl to take the berries at the end?

(A) The tree does not want the frost to kill the berries.
(B) The birds keep eating the berries.
(C) The berries have made the tree's branches droop.
(D) The leaves have all fallen off the tree.
(E) The tree is afraid.

3. In what season does this poem begin?

(A) the dead of winter
(B) the beginning of fall
(C) the beginning of spring
(D) the middle of summer
(E) cannot be determined

4. The word "boughs" most nearly means

(A) roots
(B) leaves
(C) berries
(D) ground
(E) branches

Math section

Math practice

TIME YOURSELF – THESE PROBLEMS SHOULD TAKE YOU ABOUT 9 MINUTES TOTAL

1. If Q is the least integer greater than 3.5, what is Q?

   (A) 3
   (B) 4
   (C) 5
   (D) 6
   (E) 7

2. A lamp is on sale for $80. This is 20% off of the original price. What was the original price?

   (A) $60
   (B) $64
   (C) $70
   (D) $80
   (E) $100

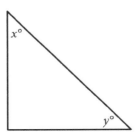

3. If the triangle above is a right triangle and $x = y$, what is the value of x?

   (A) 30
   (B) 40
   (C) 45
   (D) 60
   (E) 90

4. Of the following, which CANNOT be written in the form $(3 \times Q) + 4$, where Q is a whole number?

   (A) 10
   (B) 16
   (C) 19
   (D) 25
   (E) 27

5. Peter is drawing a rectangle where the length and width will be whole integers. If he wants the perimeter to be 30 cm and he wants the length to be twice the width, which of the following would be the area of his rectangle?

   (A) 10 cm²
   (B) 20 cm²
   (C) 30 cm²
   (D) 40 cm²
   (E) 50 cm²

6. If $16 - x + 8 = 3x$, then what is the value of x?

   (A) 2
   (B) 3
   (C) 6
   (D) 9
   (E) 12

7. A circle with a radius of 7 is inscribed in a square.

   What is the area of the shaded region?

   (A) $49 - 7\pi$
   (B) $49 - 49\pi$
   (C) $96 - 49\pi$
   (D) $196 - 49\pi$
   (E) $196 - 196\pi$

Workout #12 Answers

Vocabulary

Roots

1. opposite of or away from
2. to cut
3. trust or faith
4. all
5. to speak
6. big
7. good or well
8. time
9. believe
10. bad
11. well or good
12. new
13. life
14. to break
15. join
16. group or to gather
17. to teach
18. to send
19. ask or seek
20. empty

Verbal section

Synonyms practice

1. C – This is a word to remember from Workout #5. Study your flashcards if you missed this one!

2. B – Did you notice how congeal and coagulate both start with "co"? This is not a coincidence. Congeal and coagulate both mean to thicken.

3. A – Meticulous means to pay close attention to detail, but you may not have known that scrupulous also means the same thing. However, unhappy, stable, and funky are easy to rule out (choices B, C, and E). You may not have known choices A and D, but querulous does have the "quer" root which means to question. That makes it easy to rule out choice D and choose A.

4. E – This is a word to remember from Workout #10, be sure to study your flashcards if you missed this one.

5. D – This is a word to remember from Workout #8.

Analogies practice

1. B – Tactful and offensive are antonyms. Proud and dismayed are also antonyms. Even if you don't know what dismayed means, you can rule out the other answer choices. Choices D and E have unrelated words (practice can lead to being accomplished, but it doesn't always). Choices A and C have words that are similar in meaning. Therefore, we are left with choice B.

2. A – Obsolete is a characteristic of a phonograph. A marathoner must be athletic by definition. No one can run 26 miles who is not athletic!

3. C – A door is how you enter a house. A hatch is how you enter a submarine. If you didn't know what hatch meant, it could have been tempting to choose window is to wall since a window is a hole in the wall, or stairway is to basement since a stairway is how you go to the basement. However, you would have to do some real convincing to agree that these are the same relationships as door is to house. If you have to try that hard, you have just talked yourself into the wrong answer.

4. D –A prologue is at the beginning of a book and the epilogue is at the end. This is the same relationship as introduction and conclusion.

5. E – Euphoria means extreme happiness and malaise is misery. The "eu" root means well or good and the "mal" root means bad, so we know the relationship must be antonyms. Precision and error are also antonyms.

Reading section

Reading practice

1. B – The tree's branches bend, but there is no evidence that the whole tree dies. The birds are singing, but the poem does not mention them leaving. However, the tree has just leaves at first, and then blossoms, and then berries, so we can assume that the seasons changed.

2. C – The poem says "as it bent / Its full boughs to her feet" is another way to say that the branches were drooping.

3. C – The tree is still green in the beginning and there are not yet blossoms. This occurs during early spring.

4. E – Boughs is a synonym for branches – think of the Christmas song "deck the halls with boughs of holly".

Math section

Math practice

1. B – An integer has to be a whole number, not a fraction. The smallest whole number that is bigger than 3.5 is 4.

2. E – If the lamp is on sale for $80, then the original price must have been greater than $80. Choice E is the only answer choice that works.

3. C – If it is a right triangle, then the two non-right angles must add to 90. Also, since $x = y$, we know that they must be 45 degrees each in order to add to 90.

4. E – What this question is asking you to do is to figure out which answer choice could be equal to $(3 \times Q) + 4$, where Q is a whole number. We set each answer choice equal to $(3 \times Q) + 4$ and solve for Q.

If we do choice A:

$$(3 \times Q) + 4 = 10$$
$$ -4 \quad -4$$
$$3Q = 6$$
$$Q = 2$$

Since the question is asking which answer choice would NOT give us a whole number, choice A is out. We can see that we are looking for answer choice where we can subtract 4 and get a number that is NOT divisible by 3. 27 is the only answer choice that works. (If we subtract 4 from 27 we get 23, which is not divisible by 3.)

5. E – Let's make the width equal to x. This makes the length equal to $2x$. To find the perimeter, we do:

$$x + 2x + x + 2x = 6x$$

We know that the perimeter is equal to 30, so we set $6x$ equal to 30. That gives us 5 for x. We therefore know that the width is 5 and the length is 10.

$Area = width \times length = 5 \times 10 = 50$. Choice E is correct.

6. C – Our first step here is to combine like terms. If we do that, we get $24 - x = 3x$. Now we can add x to both sides and get $24 = 4x$. Therefore, x must equal 6, or answer choice C.

7. D – For shaded region problems, we always have to find the area of a larger shape and then subtract off the area of the region that is not shaded. Since the circle is inscribed in the square, the side length of the square is equal to the diameter of the circle. This means that the side length of the square must be twice the radius, or 14. If we multiply 14×14, we find that the area of the square is 196. This allows us to eliminate choices A, B, and C. If we look at the remaining choices, choice D correctly subtracts off the area of the circle (the unshaded region) so that we are left with just the shaded region.

Vocabulary

Roots

Below are some roots. I will give you the definition of each root and then two examples of words that have that root. Look up the meanings of those words and write the definitions in the blanks provided. As you look up the definition of each word, think about how it relates to the root. After you write the definition of each word, write a sentence using the word or a memory trick or association for remembering the word.

Root: *amb / ambul*
  Definition – to walk or go
Examples:
  Amble
    Definition:
    Sentence or memory trick:
  Circumambulate
    Definition:
    Sentence or memory trick:

Root: *bell / belli*
  Definition – war
Examples:
  Belligerent
    Definition:
    Sentence or memory trick:
  Bellicose
    Definition:
    Sentence or memory trick:

Word to remember!

Wily – cunning and willing to use trickery

Example: The Wil. E. Coyote was very wily indeed when he tricked the roadrunner into running off the cliff once again.

Now, MAKE FLASHCARDS FOR ALL THE WORDS ABOVE – AND STUDY THEM!

Verbal section

Synonyms practice

TIME YOURSELF – THESE QUESTIONS SHOULD TAKE ABOUT 3 MINUTES.

1. MISSIVE:

   (A) inquest
   (B) junction
   (C) animal
   (D) letter
   (E) aggregation

2. AMBULATORY:

   (A) migratory
   (B) fascinating
   (C) vacant
   (D) inquisitive
   (E) profound

3. WILY:

   (A) fast
   (B) crafty
   (C) delinquent
   (D) frugal
   (E) lazy

4. ACQUISITION:

   (A) question
   (B) doctrine
   (C) chronicle
   (D) benefit
   (E) possession

5. CREED:

   (A) content
   (B) monotone
   (C) doctrine
   (D) diplomat
   (E) descent

Analogies practice

TIME YOURSELF – THESE QUESTIONS SHOULD TAKE LESS THAN 3 MINUTES.

1. Docile is to belligerent as

   (A) harmonious is to mellifluous
   (B) harsh is to rancorous
   (C) gregarious is to antisocial
   (D) benign is to harmless
   (E) innovative is to technology

2. Tact is to emissary as

   (A) rudeness is to conductor
   (B) flavor is to licorice
   (C) plan is to battle
   (D) agility is to gymnast
   (E) mission is to spy

3. Euphony is to sound as

   (A) fragrant is to smell
   (B) loud is to riot
   (C) soft is to floor
   (D) compassionate is to priest
   (E) messy is to room

4. Ewe is to lamb as

   (A) goose is to duck
   (B) stallion is to pony
   (C) tadpole is to minnow
   (D) tiger is to lion
   (E) cow is to calf

5. Wrench is to tighten as

   (A) hammer is to hang
   (B) saw is to cut
   (C) drill is to screw
   (D) wood is to tree
   (E) count is to numbers

Reading section

Reading practice

Below is a practice reading passage. It is a non-fiction passage.

TIME YOURSELF – THIS PASSAGE AND QUESTIONS SHOULD TAKE A TOTAL OF 5 MINUTES

Although he did not invent production line assembly, Henry Ford was the first industrialist to use it on a large scale. Before the popularization of the production line, most goods were handcrafted by a person who would perform every step of assembly from start to finished product. Between 1908 and 1915, Line 5 Henry Ford set up factories that were radically different, however. In his factories, each person was responsible for just one step of the process. This minimized the time that workers spent switching tools or looking for parts. He also used interchangeable parts so that they could be mass produced rather than fitted for each individual car.

10   Henry Ford once used his large factories to produce the Model T car. This new process of assembly line production allowed Ford to produce a better car in less time. These factors allowed Ford to sell the car for less, which created more buyers as more people could afford his cars. It also allowed him to pay his workers higher wages. When other companies saw the immense profits that Henry Ford 15   realized through assembly line production, it became the standard for many different industries.

1. This passage is primarily about

    (A) the life of Henry Ford
    (B) industrialization in the early 20th century
    (C) the development of assembly line production
    (D) the importance of the Model T
    (E) how factories work today

2. According to the passage, one of the reasons that the Model T was so successful was that

    (A) mass production produced a more attractive car
    (B) of the people who could afford cars, more of them preferred the Model T than other models not produced on an assembly line
    (C) the workers who made the Model T were paid more
    (D) it was less expensive than other cars
    (E) it had a longer lasting engine than other cars

3. This passage would most likely be found in

    (A) an encyclopedia
    (B) a current news item
    (C) a car manufacturing manual
    (D) the diary of Henry Ford
    (E) a photojournal

4. The author's attitude toward assembly line production can best be described as

    (A) disgust
    (B) awe
    (C) ambivalence
    (D) admiration
    (E) skepticism

5. What does the author mean by "interchangeable parts" (line 8)?

    (A) parts that were made to fit just one car
    (B) parts that were made to fit in any car of the same model
    (C) parts that were handcrafted
    (D) parts that could be used on any part of the car
    (E) parts that were meant to last a long time

Math section

Math practice

TIME YOURSELF – THESE PROBLEMS SHOULD TAKE YOU ABOUT 9 MINUTES TOTAL

1. Which of the following is closest to .24 × 41?

    (A) $\frac{1}{4}$ of 40

    (B) $\frac{1}{4}$ of 44

    (C) $\frac{1}{2}$ of 40

    (D) $\frac{1}{2}$ of 44

    (E) 4 divided by 40

2. If $\frac{1}{2}$ of a number is less than 16, than the number CANNOT be

    (A) less than 32

    (B) equal to 32

    (C) less than 8

    (D) equal to 8

    (E) equal to zero

3. If a hollow plastic tube (shown above) is placed on a piece of paper, which picture represents all the points where the tube touches the paper?

(A)

(B)

(C)

(D)

(E)

4. In a particular city, out of every 1,000 homes, 2.5 of them have a dog. If there are 2 million homes, how many of them have a dog?

(A) 5
(B) 50
(C) 500
(D) 5,000
(E) 50,000

5. If x, y, and z are consecutive numbers, which of the following must be true?

(A) xyz must be positive
(B) xyz must be negative
(C) $x + y + z$ cannot equal zero
(D) $x + y$ is greater than z
(E) none of the above

6. What is the slope of a line that is perpendicular to $3x + 6y = 5$?

   (A) -2

   (B) $-\dfrac{1}{2}$

   (C) $\dfrac{1}{2}$

   (D) 1

   (E) 2

7. The volume of a cylinder is 288π cm^3 and its height is 8 cm. This cylinder is going to be placed inside a box that is a rectangular prism. What are the smallest dimensions of a box that the cylinder would fit inside?

   (A) 6 cm × 6 cm × 8 cm

   (B) 6 cm × 8 cm × 8 cm

   (C) 8 cm × 8 cm × 6 cm

   (D) 12 cm × 12 cm × 8 cm

   (E) 18 cm × 2 cm × 8 cm

Workout #13 Answers

Vocabulary

Look them up!

Verbal section

Synonyms practice

1. D – The "mis" / "mit" root means to send. You send a letter, so choice D is correct.

2. A – The "amb" root means to walk or go, so migratory describes a person or animal that moves around frequently (think of a bird migrating).

3. B – This one is a little tricky because crafty does not mean good at crafts. Crafty means scheming, or wily.

4. E – To acquire something is to get it, or to take it into your possession. An acquisition is something that you have acquired, or a possession.

5. C – Creed comes from the "cred" root, which means to believe. A doctrine is also something that you believe in (a doctrine is a set of beliefs that is usually pretty strict).

Analogies practice

1. C – Docile and belligerent are antonyms (docile means calm and belligerent means looking for a fight – do you see the "bell" root?). Using roots, we can see that gregarious and antisocial are also antonyms. "Greg" means to gather, but "anti" means not, so antisocial means not social.

2. D – Tact is a characteristic of an emissary (an emissary is someone that one country sends to another country to build relations). Agility is a characteristic of a gymnast (agility is flexibility, so by definition a gymnast must be agile).

3. A – Euphony is a pleasant sound ("eu" means well or good and "phon" means sound). Fragrant is a pleasant smell.

4. E – A ewe is a female sheep and a lamb is a baby sheep. A ewe produces a lamb. A cow is a female that produces a calf.

5. B – A wrench is used to tighten. A saw is used to cut. Don't be fooled by choices A and C. You might use a hammer to hang a picture, but if you were asked the primary use for a hammer, would you say "to hang"? And while a drill is used to make a hole so that you can screw, it is a screwdriver's job to screw and not a drill's.

Reading section
Reading practice

1. C – If we look at the last sentence, we can see that the passage is about assembly line construction. The passage does mention Henry Ford and the Model T, but neither of those is the main idea.

2. D – The passage reads, "These factors allowed Ford to sell the car for less". This gives us evidence for choice D. There is simply no evidence in the passage for choices A, B, or E. For choice C, the passage does state that Ford could pay his workers higher wages, but there is no evidence given that this made the Model T successful.

3. A – This passage gives us a summary, which is what an encyclopedia article does. It wouldn't be a current news item because assembly line production was developed a long time ago. It wouldn't be in a manual because a manual gives step-by-step instructions. A diary would be personal in tone and a photojournal would be just pictures. We are left with choice A.

4. D – The tone is definitely positive. That leaves us with choices B and D. The word "awe", however, is strongly positive and too extreme for a passage on this test. Admiration is positive but not over the top, so choice D is correct.

5. B – The passage says that interchangeable parts "could be mass produced rather than fitted for each individual car". Choice B restates this.

Math section
Math practice

1. A – .24 can be rounded off to $\frac{1}{4}$ and 41 can be rounded to 40. Choice A is correct.

2. B – We can translate "$\frac{1}{2}$ of a number is less than 16" into an inequality:

$$\frac{1}{2}x < 16$$

To get x by itself, we multiply both sides by 2. This gives us:

$$x < 32$$

Since we are looking for the answer that CANNOT work, choice B is correct. The number has to be less than 32, not equal to 32.

3. A – The problem tells us that the tube is hollow, so we can rule out choices B and D. This problem is basically asking us to translate between a 3-D picture and a 2-D picture. In the 3-D picture, the bottom looks like an oval, but that is how we represent a circle in 3-D in order to show depth. A tube is actually round, so choice A is correct.

4. D – We can set up equivalent fractions to solve this one:

$$\frac{2.5}{1,000} = \frac{x}{2,000,000}$$

Since we are not allowed to use a calculator on this test, our first step will be to multiply both sides by 1,000 so we can get rid of some of those zeros. That leaves us with:

$$\frac{2.5}{1} = \frac{x}{2,000}$$

When we cross-multiply, we get:

$$2.5 \times 2,000 = x$$

When we do the math, we get that there are 5,000 homes with dogs, or choice D.

5. E – Since this is a must be true problem, we need to plug in our own numbers to try to disprove each answer choice. If we plug in -1, 0, and 1, we get that $xyz = 0$. This allows us to rule out choices A and B since zero is neither positive nor negative. This also makes $x + y + z = 0$, so we can rule out choice C. Also, $x + y = -1$, which is not greater than z (1), so choice D is out. That leaves us with choice E.

6. E – In order to answer this question, we need to remember that the slopes of perpendicular lines are negative reciprocals of one another. If we rearrange the equation given ($3x + 6y = 5$) into slope intercept form ($y = mx + b$), then we can easily see the slope of the line given. The math looks like this:

$$3x + 6y = 5$$
$${-3x} \quad {-3x}$$
$$6y = -3x + 5$$
$$\div 6 \quad \div 6$$
$$y = -\frac{1}{2}x + \frac{5}{6}$$

We can see that the slope of the line given is $-\frac{1}{2}$. Since the negative reciprocal of $-\frac{1}{2}$ is 2, answer choice E is correct.

7. D – We need to work backwards from what we are given. The question tells us that the volume of the cylinder is 288π cm^3 and that the height is 8 cm. We can use the formula volume of cylinder $= \pi r^2 h$. Now we plug in the information that we have and then solve for what we don't (the radius):

$$288\pi = \pi r^2 \times 8$$
$$\div 8\pi \quad \div 8\pi$$
$$36 = r^2$$
$$6 = r$$

Now that we know the radius and the height, we can figure out the smallest dimensions of a box that could contain the cylinder. If the radius is 6, then the diameter is 12. This means that the box must be $12 \times 12 \times 8$ in order to contain the cylinder.

Vocabulary

Roots

Below are some roots. I will give you the definition of each root and then two examples of words that have that root. Look up the meanings of those words and write the definitions in the blanks provided. As you look up the definition of each word, think about how it relates to the root. After you write the definition of each word, write a sentence using the word or a memory trick or association for remembering the word.

Root: *cert*
    Definition – sure
Examples:
    Ascertain
        Definition:
        Sentence or memory trick:
    Certify
        Definition:
        Sentence or memory trick:

Root: *mon*
    Definition – advise
Examples:
    Remonstrance
        Definition:
        Sentence or memory trick:
    Admonish
        Definition:
        Sentence or memory trick:

Word to remember!

Capricious – unpredictable or impulsive

Example: Many young celebrities are known for their capricious behavior; they have a new boyfriend and a new hair color every week.

Now, MAKE FLASHCARDS FOR ALL THE WORDS ABOVE – AND STUDY THEM!

Verbal section

Synonyms practice

TIME YOURSELF – THESE QUESTIONS SHOULD TAKE ABOUT 3 MINUTES.

1. WILY:

    (A) ambulatory
    (B) certain
    (C) crowded
    (D) cunning
    (E) gregarious

2. ASCERTAIN:

    (A) determine
    (B) question
    (C) accuse
    (D) dismiss
    (E) disprove

3. SOMNAMBULATE:

    (A) remit
    (B) sleepwalk
    (C) freeze
    (D) covet
    (E) rebel

4. INQUEST:

(A) malady

(B) defense

(C) investigation

(D) trial

(E) eulogy

5. INTERMITTENT:

(A) content

(B) novel

(C) benevolent

(D) tactful

(E) sporadic

Analogies practice

TIME YOURSELF – THESE QUESTIONS SHOULD TAKE LESS THAN 3 MINUTES.

1. Preamble is to conclusion as

(A) prologue is to epilogue

(B) chapter is to book

(C) author is to writing

(D) book is to store

(E) fiction is to nonfiction

2. Certain is to unsure as

(A) confident is to athletic

(B) solid is to plain

(C) magnanimous is to benevolent

(D) difficult is to docile

(E) gregarious is to funny

3. Vacant is to occupants as

(A) frustrated is to anger

(B) quiet is to noise

(C) frank is to politics

(D) fortunate is to wealth

(E) fantastic is to clean

4. Question is to exam as

   (A) quiz is to test
   (B) front is to back
   (C) inquiry is to attack
   (D) sock is to foot
   (E) note is to song

5. Mislead is to defraud as

   (A) lie is to certify
   (B) last is to crumble
   (C) object is to rebel
   (D) fume is to consider
   (E) collide is to fracture

Reading section

Reading practice

Below is a practice reading passage. It is from an essay by Arthur Christopher Benson.

TIME YOURSELF – THIS PASSAGE AND QUESTIONS SHOULD TAKE A TOTAL OF 5 MINUTES

> There are many motives that impel us to travel, to change our sky, as Horace calls it—good motives and bad, selfish and unselfish, noble and ignoble. With some people it is pure restlessness; the tedium of ordinary life weighs on them, and travel, they think, will distract them; people travel for the sake of health, or for business reasons, or to accompany someone else, or because other people travel. And these motives are neither good nor bad, they are simply sufficient. Some people travel to enlarge their minds, or to write a book; and the worst of travelling for such reasons is that it so often implants in the traveler, when he returns, a desperate desire to enlarge other people's minds too. Unhappily, it needs an extraordinary gift of vivid description and a tactful art of selection to make the reflections of one's travels interesting to other people.

Line 5

10

1. The author implies that most writing about travelling

   (A) is well written
   (B) bores the reader
   (C) sells well in bookstores
   (D) lacks enough detail
   (E) is well received by the press

2. This passage is primarily about

   (A) Horace
   (B) specific travels that the author has taken
   (C) the history of travel writing
   (D) the reasons that people travel and write about it
   (E) what makes good travel writing

3. In the passage, all of the following reasons are given for travelling EXCEPT

   (A) the dullness of routine life
   (B) well-being
   (C) migration
   (D) monetary gains
   (E) education

4. The author's tone can best be described as

   (A) humorous
   (B) malicious
   (C) ambivalent
   (D) bitter
   (E) rowdy

Math section

Math practice

TIME YOURSELF – THESE PROBLEMS SHOULD TAKE YOU ABOUT 9 MINUTES TOTAL

1. Which of the following is greater than $\frac{1}{2}$?

   (A) $\frac{9}{20}$

   (B) $\frac{16}{33}$

   (C) $\frac{101}{202}$

   (D) $\frac{8}{15}$

   (E) $\frac{12}{25}$

2. There are 14 students in Ms. Smith's class. They sold an average of 4 rolls of wrapping paper per student for the school fundraiser. How many rolls did they sell in total?

   (A) 4

   (B) 14

   (C) 28

   (D) 36

   (E) 56

3. The population of a town increased from 3,500 in 1990 to 7 million in 2010. How many times greater was the population in 2010 than in 1990?

   (A) 100

   (B) 200

   (C) 500

   (D) 2,000

   (E) 20,000

4. If $q = 3r + 7$, what does $q - 2$ equal?

    (A) $3r + 9$

    (B) $3r + 5$

    (C) $6r + 7$

    (D) $6r + 5$

    (E) It cannot be determined by information given

5. In a particular school, $\frac{1}{3}$ of the students walk, $\frac{1}{6}$ of them are driven by their parents, and the remainder ride the bus. If four students are driven by their parents, how many students ride the bus?

    (A) 4

    (B) 6

    (C) 8

    (D) 12

    (E) 16

6. Combine and simplify the expression $(2m^4 + 3m^2 - m + 5) - (m^4 - 8m^3 - m - 6)$

    (A) $m^4 + 8m^3 + 3m^2 + 11$

    (B) $m^4 - 8m^3 + 3m^2 + 11$

    (C) $m^4 - 8m^3 + 3m^2 - 2m + 11$

    (D) $m^4 - 8m^3 + 3m^2 - 2m - 1$

    (E) $3m^4 + 8m^3 + 3m^2 - 2m + 11$

7. If q is an integer between 2 and 24, what is the probability that q is divisible by 3 but not by 4?

    (A) $\dfrac{5}{23}$

    (B) $\dfrac{6}{23}$

    (C) $\dfrac{5}{21}$

    (D) $\dfrac{6}{21}$

    (E) $\dfrac{5}{24}$

Workout #14 Answers

Vocabulary

Look them up!

Verbal section

Synonyms practice

1. D – This is a word to remember from Workout #13, so study your flashcards if you missed this one.
2. A – The "cert" root means sure, so to ascertain is to make sure, or to determine.
3. B – "Amb" means to walk or go, and sleepwalk is the only answer choice that captures this meaning ("somn" means to sleep).
4. C – The "ques" root means to ask or to seek. An inquest seeks answers and so does an investigation.
5. E – Intermittent means off and on (or not steady) and so does sporadic.

Analogies practice

1. A – A preamble comes before a piece of writing and the conclusion comes at the end, so this is a sequence relationship. A prologue comes at the beginning of the book and the epilogue comes at the end, so choice A is correct.
2. D – Certain and unsure are antonyms. Choices A, B, and E have words that are unrelated. Choice C has synonyms. Only choice D has antonyms.
3. B – Vacant means without occupants. Quiet means without noise.
4. E – Questions make up an exam and notes make up a song.
5. C – This is a degree relationship. To mislead is to let someone believe something that is not true, but to defraud is to mislead someone with malicious intentions. To object is to think that another person is wrong, to rebel is to think that they are so wrong that you act out against them. The trick to this one is knowing that the word "object" has more than one meaning. It can be a noun or a verb.

Reading section

Reading practice

1. B – If we look at the last sentence of the passage, the author says that it is very hard to make travel writing "interesting to other people". This idea is restated in choice B.

2. D – The first half of the passage talks about why people travel and the second half talks about why people write about it. Choice D restates this.

3. C – There is evidence for all of the answer choices except choice C.

4. A – The author seems to be sharing a joke with us, so the tone is humorous. Students can have trouble identifying when adults are trying to be funny, though, so ruling out may be the best strategy on this question. Malicious, bitter, and rowdy are all too extreme for the SSAT. Ambivalence means that an author can't decide whether something is good or bad, which is not the case in this passage. We are left with humorous.

Math section

Math practice

1. D – To answer this question, we can write fractions that are equivalent to $\frac{1}{2}$ next to each answer choice and then compare.

Answer choice	Equal to $\frac{1}{2}$	Which is greater?
(A) $\dfrac{9}{20}$	$\dfrac{10}{20}$	$\dfrac{1}{2}$
(B) $\dfrac{16}{33}$	$\dfrac{16}{32}$	$\dfrac{1}{2}$
(C) $\dfrac{101}{202}$	$\dfrac{101}{202}$	Equal
(D) $\dfrac{8}{15}$	$\dfrac{8}{16}$	Answer choice
(E) $\dfrac{12}{25}$	$\dfrac{12}{24}$	$\dfrac{1}{2}$

Only answer choice D is greater than $\frac{1}{2}$.

2. E – We can rearrange the equation $average = sum \div number\ of\ numbers$ to get $average \times number\ of\ numbers = sum$. If we plug the numbers from our problem into this equation, we get $sum = 4 \times 14 = 56$ rolls of wrapping paper.

3. D – We can set up the equation:

$$3{,}500x = 7{,}000{,}000$$

To make our life easier, the first thing to do is divide both sides by 100 to get rid of some of those zeroes. We are left with:

$$35x = 70{,}000$$

Now we can divide both sides by 35 to get $x = 2{,}000$, so the correct answer is choice D.

4. B – In order to get $q - 2$, we have to subtract 2 from each side. This gives us:

$$q - 2 = 3r + 7 - 2 = 3r + 5$$

Choice B is correct.

5. D – To solve this problem, we need to give all of the fractions a common denominator, which in this case is 6. Since $\frac{1}{3} = \frac{2}{6}$, we know that $\frac{2}{6}$ of the students walk and $\frac{1}{6}$ of the students are driven, which leaves $\frac{3}{6}$ of the students to ride the bus. If 4 students are driven and they represent $\frac{1}{6}$ of the school, then there must be 8 students who walk ($\frac{2}{6}$ of the school), and 12 students who ride the bus ($\frac{3}{6}$ of the school). Choice D is correct.

6. A – The keys to this question are to remember the rules for combining like terms and to remember to distribute the minus sign to all of the elements in the second set of parentheses. First let's go ahead and distribute that minus sign:

$$(2m^4 + 3m^2 - m + 5) - (m^4 - 8m^3 - m - 6)$$
$$= 2m^4 + 3m^2 - m + 5 - m^4 + 8m^3 + m + 6$$

Now let's rearrange so that our like terms are grouped. The key is to remember that we must take the sign before each term with it when we move terms around.

$$2m^4 - m^4 + 8m^3 + 3m^2 - m + m + 5 + 6$$

Now it is easy to combine like terms and we get $m^4 + 8m^3 + 3m^2 + 11$.

7. D – In order to find a probability, we first have to figure out how many total events there could be. There are 21 numbers BETWEEN 2 and 24, so 21 becomes the denominator in our probability (we have to remember that "between" does not include the numbers 2 and 24 themselves). Now we have to figure out how many of those numbers are divisible by 3. The numbers 3, 6, 9, 12, 15, 18, and 21 are between 2 and 24 and divisible by 3. Now we have to eliminate any of these numbers that are also divisible by 4. Since 12 is divisible by 4, we have to take it out of our list. We are left with 6 numbers $(3, 6, 9, 15, 18, 21)$ that match the desired outcome, so the probability is $\dfrac{6}{21}$.

Workout #15

Vocabulary

Roots

Below are some roots. I will give you the definition of each root and then two examples of words that have that root. Look up the meanings of those words and write the definitions in the blanks provided. As you look up the definition of each word, think about how it relates to the root. After you write the definition of each word, write a sentence using the word or a memory trick or association for remembering the word.

Root: *pel*
    Definition – drive
Examples:
    Propel
        Definition:
        Sentence or memory trick:
    Expel
        Definition:
        Sentence or memory trick:

Root: *tort / tors*
    Definition – twist
Examples:
    Contort
        Definition:
        Sentence or memory trick:
    Tortuous
        Definition:
        Sentence or memory trick:

Word to remember!

Sporadic – not happening regularly

Example: He was not the most committed player on the team; his attendance at practice was sporadic.

Now, MAKE FLASHCARDS FOR ALL THE WORDS ABOVE – AND STUDY THEM!

Verbal section

Synonyms practice

TIME YOURSELF – THESE QUESTIONS SHOULD TAKE ABOUT 3 MINUTES.

1. CAPRICIOUS:

    (A) impulsive
    (B) fair
    (C) stunning
    (D) weary
    (E) grumpy

2. RENDEZVOUS:

    (A) lousy timing
    (B) long drive
    (C) morbid fascination
    (D) secret meeting
    (E) slow healing

3. PREMONITION:

    (A) depth
    (B) forewarning
    (C) stalemate
    (D) scruples
    (E) negotiation

4. DEMISE:

   (A) dispatch
   (B) vitality
   (C) assistance
   (D) progress
   (E) termination

5. VACUOUS:

   (A) constructive
   (B) petty
   (C) empty
   (D) concise
   (E) proud

Analogies practice

TIME YOURSELF – THESE QUESTIONS SHOULD TAKE LESS THAN 3 MINUTES.

1. Propel is to stop as

   (A) expel is to limit
   (B) fund is to spend
   (C) aggregate is to segregate
   (D) monitor is to watch
   (E) malign is to deter

2. Contort is to bend as

   (A) deplete is to use up
   (B) stifle is to encourage
   (C) finish is to begin
   (D) grate is to enjoy
   (E) grasp is to destroy

3. Satellite is to orbit as

   (A) earth is to moon
   (B) rocket is to propulsion
   (C) comedian is to laugh
   (D) galaxy is to Milky Way
   (E) racecar is to track

4. Peaceful is to sanctuary as

   (A) calm is to ocean
   (B) ornate is to ballroom
   (C) clean is to gym
   (D) sloppy is to student
   (E) furnished is to studio

5. Soothe is to exacerbate as

   (A) force is to contain
   (B) smile is to grin
   (C) amble is to walk
   (D) rebel is to obey
   (E) certify is to inquire

Reading section

Reading practice

On the following page is a practice reading passage. It is from Marco Paul's Adventures in Pursuit of Knowledge.

TIME YOURSELF – THIS PASSAGE AND QUESTIONS SHOULD TAKE A TOTAL OF 6 MINUTES

One summer, Forester and Marco Paul formed a plan for going to Quebec. Marco was very much interested in going to Quebec, as he wanted to see the fortifications. Forester had told him that Quebec was a strongly-fortified city, being a military post of great importance, belonging to the British government.

Line 5 Marco was very much pleased at the idea of seeing the fortifications, and the soldiers that he supposed must be placed there to defend them.

On their way to Quebec, they had to sail up the Kennebec in a steamboat. As they were passing along, Marco and Forester sat upon the deck. It was a pleasant summer morning. They had been sailing all night upon the sea, on the

10 route from Boston to the mouth of the Kennebec. They entered the mouth of the Kennebec very early in the morning, just before Forester and Marco got up. And thus it happened that when they came up upon the deck, they found that they were sailing in a river. The water was smooth and glassy, shining brilliantly under the rays of the morning sun, which was just beginning to rise.

15 The shores of the river were rocky and barren. Here and there, in the coves and eddies, were what appeared to Marco to be little fences in the water. Forester told him that they were for catching fish. The steamboat moved very slowly, and every moment the little bell would ring, and the engine would stop. Then the boat would move more slowly still, until the bell sounded again for the engine to be put

20 in motion, and then the boat would go on a little faster.

"What makes them keep stopping?" said Marco.

"The water is very low this morning," said Forester, "and they have to proceed very carefully, or else they will get aground."

"What makes the water so low now?" asked Marco.

25 "There are two reasons," replied Forester. "It is late in the summer, and the streams and springs are all low; so that there is but little water to come down from the country above. Then, besides, the tide is low this morning in the sea, and that causes what water there is in the bed of the river to run off into the sea."

"Is not there any tide in the river?" asked Marco.

30 "No," said Forester, "I suppose there is not, strictly speaking. That is, the moon, which attracts the waters of the ocean, and makes them rise and fall in succession, produces no sensible effect upon the waters of a river. But then the rise and fall of the sea itself causes all rivers to rise and fall near their mouths, and as far up as the influence of the sea extends. You see, in fact, that it must be so."

1. It can be inferred from the passage that Marco

    (A) has run away from home
    (B) is interested in the military
    (C) is a sailor
    (D) frequently travels to Quebec
    (E) is a scientist by profession

2. According to the passage, tides affect rivers

    (A) not at all
    (B) only in the spring and summer
    (C) along the whole length of the river
    (D) only near where the river meets the sea
    (E) only in the Northern hemisphere

3. According to the passage, a bell rings in order to

    (A) warn the steamboat captain that the water was too shallow to keep the engine running
    (B) wake the passengers
    (C) let the fishermen know when a fish had been caught in the fences
    (D) let the soldiers in Quebec know that a boat was approaching
    (E) warn the captain that there was a high tide

4. Marco and Forester's journey can best be described as

    (A) harrowing
    (B) dangerous
    (C) long
    (D) pleasant
    (E) boring

5. A good title for this piece would be:

    (A) "Ninety Days to Quebec: A Rough Journey"
    (B) "A Journey up the Kennebec"
    (C) "Early fortifications in Quebec"
    (D) "Two Boys on the Loose"
    (E) "A History of the Kennebec River"

Math section

Math practice

TIME YOURSELF – THESE PROBLEMS SHOULD TAKE YOU ABOUT 9 MINUTES TOTAL

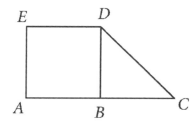

1. If $ABDE$ is a square and AB is equal in length to BC, which of the following paths is the longest?

    (A) A to B to D to E
    (B) A to E to D to B
    (C) B to D to E to A
    (D) A to E to D to C
    (E) C to B to A to E

2. Which of the following is 3.03 closest to?

    (A) 3
    (B) 3.3
    (C) 3.4
    (D) 4
    (E) 30

3. If $3 + (A + B) = 10$, and B is greater than zero, which of the following could A NOT be?

    (A) 7
    (B) 6
    (C) 3.3
    (D) 2
    (E) 0

A   B   C   D

4. In the figure above, the distance from A to C is 30 and the distance from A to B is half the distance from B to C. If the distance from A to D is 40, what is the distance from B to D?

(A) 40

(B) 30

(C) 20

(D) 15

(E) 10

5. Amy sent out invitations for her birthday party. On the invitations, she wrote that each person could bring up to two siblings. What is the maximum number of guests that Amy could expect if x is the number of invitations sent?

(A) x

(B) $x + 2$

(C) $2x + 2$

(D) $2x + 4$

(E) $3x$

6. In the number 256,780.19, which digit has the greatest value?

(A) 2

(B) 5

(C) 7

(D) 8

(E) 9

7. Evaluate: $\dfrac{2}{3} \times \dfrac{4}{7} \times \dfrac{7}{2}$

(A) $\dfrac{8}{42}$

(B) $\dfrac{14}{42}$

(C) $\dfrac{8}{14}$

(D) $\dfrac{7}{6}$

(E) $\dfrac{4}{3}$

Workout #15 Answers

Vocabulary

Look them up!

Verbal section

Synonyms practice

1. A – This is a word to remember from Workout #14, study your flashcards if you missed this one.

2. D – This is a word to remember from Workout #9, study your flashcards if you missed this one.

3. B – "Pre" means before and "mon" means to advise. Premonition therefore means an advisement before something happens, or a forewarning ("fore" also means before).

4. E – The root "de" means down or away and "mis" means to send. Demise is the end of something, or the termination ("term" also means to end).

5. C – The "vac" root means empty, so vacuous means empty.

Analogies practice

1. C – Propel has the roots "pro" and "pel". "Pro" is a positive root and "pel" means to drive, so propel means to drive forward, which is the opposite of stop. Aggregate is also the opposite of segregate.

2. A – Contort and bend are synonyms (did you recognize the "tort" root that means to twist?). Deplete and use up also mean the same thing.

3. E – A satellite travels in an orbit and a racecar travels on a track. Earth and moon may have been tempting because they seem to go with satellite and orbit. However, the earth does not travel in a moon.

4. B – Peaceful is a characteristic of a sanctuary. Ornate is a characteristic of a ballroom – ballrooms are not built that are not ornate.

5. D – Soothe and exacerbate are antonyms. Rebel and obey are also antonyms. (Did you see the "bell" root?)

Reading section

Reading practice

1. B – The second sentence of the passage tells us that Marco wanted to go to Quebec to see the fortifications, so we can assume that he is interested in the military. There is not evidence for the other answer choices.

2. D – The passage tells us that rivers "rise and fall near their mouths", which is another way of saying where the river meets the sea.

3. A – The passage tells us that when the bell rings the boat stops, and that the boat stops when there is danger of running aground. We can put the pieces together that the bell is warning the captain that the water is shallow.

4. C – The passage tells us that the boat moves very slowly and keeps stopping, so we can assume that the journey is long.

5. B – This passage describes going up the Kennebec River, so choice B is the best answer.

Math section

Math practice

1. D – This question is testing whether or not you recognize that the hypotenuse of a right triangle is longer than either side. All of the answer choices require you to trace three segments, but because segment DC is the hypotenuse and only choice D has segment DC in it, choice D is the longest path.

2. A – 3.03 is between 3.0 and 3.1, so answer choice A is correct. Don't be fooled by choice B, the value is very different if you take out that middle 0.

3. A – First, we have to get $A + B$ by itself. If we subtract 3 from both sides, we get that $A + B = 7$. The problem tells us that B must be greater than zero, but if A was equal to 7, then B would be zero. Therefore, A can NOT be 7, so choice A is correct.

4. B – If A to C is 30, and AB is half as long as BC, then AB has to be 10 and BC has to be 20. If AC is 30 and AD is 40, then CD must be 10. To get the distance from B to D, we add BC (20) and CD (10) and get 30, or answer choice B.

5. E – Let's plug in our own numbers since there are variables in the answer choices. If Amy invites 3 friends, then they could bring 6 siblings, and she would have a total of 9 guests. Let's plug in 3 for x and see what gives us 9. Only choice E does. By the way, if you had plugged in 2 for x, you would have gotten that both choices D and E work. If this happens, you simply plug in another number until you can rule out down to one answer choice.

6. A – This question is really testing your understanding of place value. Even though 2 by itself would have the least value, it is in the hundred thousands place so it is really worth 200,000 and has the greatest value.

7. E – The trick here is to cross-cancel rather than do a long calculation. We can cancel the 2s and the 7s since there is one of each on the top and the bottom. We are left with $\frac{4}{3}$ without doing any complicated calculations.

Appendix A – Tips for the Writing Sample

Tips for the writing sample

Please note: The writing sample on the Upper Level SSAT was updated for the 2012-2013 testing season. The advice and information in this book is up to date, but other books may not have been updated yet, so do not be alarmed if the information in this book and others does not match. You can always check *www.ssat.org* if you have any questions, since that is the official website of the SSATB.

When you take the SSAT, you will be asked to complete a writing sample. You will be given 25 minutes and two pages to write your response. You will be given a choice between an essay topic and a creative topic. The questions are relatively open-ended, giving you a lot of room to show your creativity – even if you choose the essay prompt.

So what kind of questions can you expect to see? For the essay prompt, you might see questions like:

- What would you change about your school and why?
- If you could relive one day, what day would it be and why would you want to do it over?

For the creative prompts, they might look like "story starters" that a teacher may have used in your school. The test writers will give you a starting sentence and you take it from there.
Here are some examples of what these questions could look like:

- A strange wind blew through town on that Thursday night.
- He thought long and hard before slowly opening the door.
- She had never been in an experience quite like this before.

To approach the writing sample, follow this four step plan:

Step 1: Choose topic

- There is no "right" choice when deciding between an essay or fiction prompt.
- If you are extremely creative and love playing with language, the fiction prompt is a great way to showcase this talent. This talent may not appear elsewhere on your application, so here is your chance.
- If you are great at organizing ideas and developing examples, then the essay prompt may be for you.
- If you do decide ahead of time whether to write about the creative or essay prompt, be flexible. You may get to the test, read the creative prompt and just take off with it. Alternatively, you may read the creative prompt and have nothing, but the essay prompt looks intriguing.

Step 2: Plan

- Take just a couple of minutes and plan. It will be time well spent.
- If you are writing an essay, plan out what your main point (thesis) will be and what examples you are going to use.
- If you are writing from the creative prompt, decide where your story is going. You want to build to a climax, so decide ahead of time what that will be. You don't want lots of descriptive language that goes nowhere. Decide what your problem will be and how you intend to resolve it.

Step 3: Write

- Break your writing into paragraphs – don't do a two page blob.
- If you are writing an essay topic, aim for 4-5 paragraphs (introduction, 2-3 body paragraphs, and a conclusion).
- If you choose a creative topic, remember to start new paragraphs for dialogue and to break up long descriptions.
- Write legibly. It does not have to be perfect and schools know that you are writing with a time limit, but if the admissions officers can't read what you wrote, they can't judge it.

Step 4: Edit / proofread

- Save a couple of minutes for the end to look over your work.
- You won't be able to do a major editing job where you move around sentences and rewrite portions.
- Look for where you may have left out a word or misspelled something. If a word is not legible, fix that.
- Make your marks simple and clear. If you need to take something out, just put a single line through it. Use a carat to insert words that you forgot.

The writing sample is not graded, but the schools that you apply to do receive a copy.

So, what are schools looking for?

1. **Organization**

   Schools want to see that you can organize your thoughts before writing.

   If you choose the essay topic, shoot for a 4-5 paragraph essay. There should be an introductory paragraph with a clear thesis, or main point. There should then be 2-3 body, or example, paragraphs. Each of these paragraphs should have its own, distinct theme. There should then be a concluding paragraph that ties up your ideas and then suggests what comes next. For example, if you wrote about how to improve your school, maybe you could finish up by describing how these changes could help other schools as well.

   If you choose the creative topic, there should also be structure to your story. There needs to be a problem, which builds to a climax, and then a resolution. Since you only have two pages and 25 minutes to get this done, you should know your problem before you begin to write.

2. **Word choice**

   Use descriptive language. Don't describe anything as "nice" or "good". Tell us specifically why something is nice or good. Better yet, show us and don't tell us. For example, don't just say that you would make the cafeteria nicer in your school. Tell us how you would rearrange the tables to create greater class unity and improve nutritional selections in order to improve students' academic achievement.

   Use transitions. When you switch ideas, use words such as "however", "but", "although", and "in contrast to". When you are continuing with an idea, use words such as "furthermore", "in addition", and "in summation". Writing without transition words is one of the biggest complaints of English teachers, so show the reader that you know how to use them.

3. **Creativity and development of ideas**

   It is not enough just to be able to fit your writing into the form that you were taught in school. These prompts are designed for you to show how you think. This is your chance to shine! For the creative prompts, this is your chance to come up with unique ideas. If you choose the essay topic, the readers will be looking more at how well you develop your ideas. Can you see the outcome of actions? Can you provide details that are both relevant to the essay and supportive of your thesis or main idea?

The writing sample is a place for you to showcase your writing skills. It is one more piece of information that the admissions committee will use in making their decisions.

Looking for more instruction and practice?

Check out these other titles for the Upper Level SSAT:

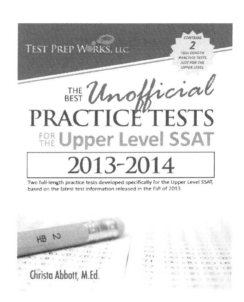

Success on the Upper Level SSAT: A Complete Course

- ✓ Strategies to use for each section of the Upper Level SSAT
- ✓ Reading and vocabulary drills
- ✓ In-depth math content instruction with practice sets
- ✓ 1 full-length practice test (different from the practice tests in *The Best Unofficial Practice Tests for the Upper Level SSAT*)

The Best Unofficial Practice Tests for the Upper Level SSAT

- ✓ 2 full-length practice tests (different from the practice test in *Success on the Upper Level SSAT*)

Made in the USA
San Bernardino, CA
26 December 2016